WELL WORTH STOPPING TO SEE

MERCER UNIVERSITY

MERCER UNIVERSITY PRESS

Endowed by

TOM WATSON BROWN
and
THE WATSON-BROWN FOUNDATION, INC.

WELL WORTH STOPPING TO SEE

ANTEBELLUM COLUMBUS, GEORGIA, THROUGH THE EYES OF TRAVELERS

MIKE BUNN

MERCER UNIVERSITY PRESS
MACON, GEORGIA

MUP/P520

Published by Mercer University Press
1400 Coleman Avenue
Macon, Georgia 31207

9 8 7 6 5 4 3 2 1

Books published by Mercer University Press are
printed on acid-free paper that meets the requirements
of the American National Standard for Information Sciences—
Permanence of Paper for Printed Library Materials.

Book design by Jim Burt / Burt&Burt

ISBN 978-0-88146-549-5

Cataloging-in-Publication Data is available from the Library of Congress

Columbus as seen from the hills on the western bank of the Chattahoochee, ca. 1840. *City of Columbus,* by James Smillie after T. Addison Richards, Collection of the Columbus Museum, Columbus, Georgia; Museum purchase made possible by the Evelyn S. and H. Wayne Patterson Fund G. 2007. *Courtesy of the Columbus Museum*

For my mother,

Betty Ann Knighton Bunn,

who inspired in me a love of learning,

indulged my curiosity about history at an early age,

and has always applauded my efforts

to combine the two as an adult.

→ PREFACE ←

This book is inspired by my longstanding interest in the beginnings of communities. How, why, and where cities form, and how a range of factors influences both their development and identities are, in my opinion, among the most intriguing stories from the past. Beginnings are, at once, moments of definition and possibility giving shape to something of an enduring nature while simultaneously sowing seeds that can lead to the development of something else entirely.

Few cities can trace their origins as precisely as Columbus, Georgia. As a planned city, rather than one that developed organically, Columbus sprang from the forest along the banks of the Chattahoochee River seemingly overnight into a fully formed urban center at the behest of the state legislature nearly two centuries ago. Even if Columbus skipped a few of the traditional incremental steps in American city-building, its early development was nonetheless marked by stages. The story of antebellum Columbus is that of a town planned for a purpose, a town that grew into the capacity that had been envisioned by its planners. From the inception of the idea of a city at the head of navigation of the Chattahoochee River, Columbus found itself shaped by economic market forces whose influences manifested themselves in not only its placement but in its settlement, character, and potential, as well. Having grown up in the Columbus area, I have long been fascinated with how that story unfolded, and I have found that the writings of those who visited the city in its first years provide a rich and enlightening commentary on its character and maturation.

This book chronicles through the eyes of a range of visitors the first quarter century of Columbus's development. Many historians have drawn on the rich archive of documents that helps us understand antebellum Columbus from the perspective of its residents, but only a few have attempted to provide the insight of those visitors not familiar with the inner workings of the city.

The few historians who have usually include only a few quotes from the most familiar of their travel narratives, and then only to further illustrate the frontier nature of Columbus's early days. Through an assemblage of visitor encounters, however, a unique and insightful perspective on early Columbus emerges.

The accounts contained in this book focus on Columbus's formative period—a time in which many of the enduring aspects of its past took shape. Unfiltered, unbiased, and unflinchingly honest if not always well-informed, these accounts paint a picture of the emerging town as it appeared at first glance. Even if they do not answer every question we may have about the young town, they certainly provide a new vantage point from which to evaluate its progress at key moments in time. Although many of the travelers who produced these narratives were only in the city for very short periods of time, I believe they, nonetheless, managed to capture some of the essence of the nascent community in their writings and enrich what is generally known about early Columbus by adding their unique perspective. While some travelers celebrate the city's successes and herald its prospects as much as any resident might have, they also remind us poignantly of its shortcomings and demonstrate that the city came about during a time when some weighty and unfortunate sagas in American history were unfolding: notably the institution of slavery and the removal of American Indians from east of the Mississippi River. Above all, these accounts help us understand the motivations, aspirations, and attitudes that propelled the transformation of Columbus in short order from a small and relatively isolated settlement to a burgeoning regional center of population and trade.

The writers featured here form an intriguing cross-section of visitors to antebellum Columbus. There are accounts from men and women, Europeans and Americans, journalists, scientists, entertainers, lawyers, academics, artists, and even a United States president. As a group they were well-educated, well-traveled, and well equipped to evaluate the scenes they witnessed in early Columbus. I have edited their accounts slightly for brevity and focus, but otherwise kept their wording and spelling as it appeared in the original texts. To these accounts I have added brief commentary, primarily biographical information on the authors but also additional information on what the authors saw and heard during their brief visits to Columbus in order to place the accounts in better context. The first of the seventeen accounts is slightly different than the others in that it is written in a more traditional essay format crafted from notes rather than being a narrative account of the birth of the city.

So why have I chosen to focus on the first twenty-five years of the city's history? I find the quarter-century mark to be a convenient benchmark for measuring a city's coming of age as, in many ways, twenty-five years is enough time to understand how a city has transitioned from a period of formation to a more mature entity. By the mid-1850s, political confrontations, and their consequences, over slavery were already publicly and privately occupying hearts and minds in Columbus and its environs, and visitors later in the decade were becoming more prone to evaluate the community through focusing more on the region and the shared peculiarities of slavery's presence rather than focusing exclusively on the city and the details of its uniqueness. The decision to conclude in 1853 is, admittedly, arbitrary, but I believe ending on this date works to focus the book on those aspects of life in the growing nineteenth-century city that most substantively impacted the city's historical narrative in the long term. Still, I have incorporated information on the closing of the city's pre-Civil War years into both the overview of the city's history that precedes the travel narratives, and in the epilogue so that readers can have a better appreciation of the antebellum era in its entirety.

Readers should know that I have chosen to focus exclusively on Columbus as defined by the original boundaries laid out in the survey of the city in 1828. This area, bordered by the Chattahoochee River on the west and south, Sixth Avenue on the east, and Seventeenth Street on the north, largely contained the city until well after the Civil War. While many of those who traveled to Columbus during the antebellum era certainly visited some of the prominent outlying estates that were as much a part of antebellum Columbus society as any establishment on Broad Street, I sought out travel narratives that gave life to the recognized core of the community that was, and is, at its heart. As there are precious few images of the city in its early years, we must look primarily to the written word for descriptions of how the place appeared and what it was really like in its founding era. It is my hope, therefore, that this book and the figurative portrait it paints will serve as a small contribution to

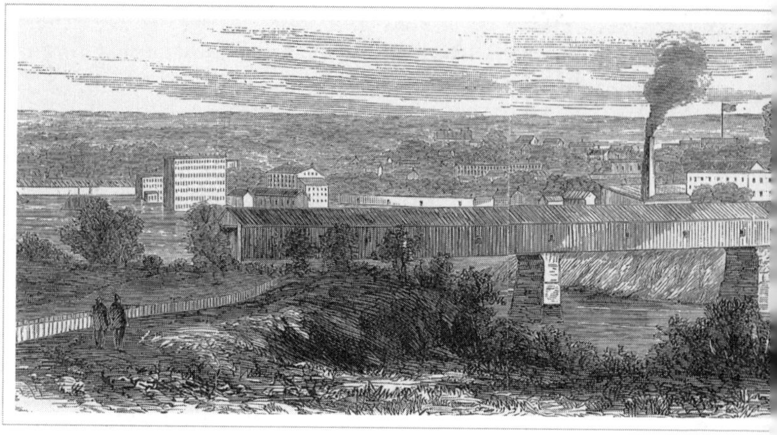

View of Columbus from Alabama, ca. 1870. *City of Columbus, Georgia* by Theodore R. Davis. Collection of the Columbus Museum, Columbus, Georgia; Museum purchase G. 1992.23. *Courtesy of the Columbus Museum.*

the rich historiography of my hometown and will entertain as much as it informs.

I am indebted to numerous individuals who have assisted me at various points during this project. First, I would like to thank Dr. Marc Jolley at Mercer University Press for his interest in the manuscript and willingness to have it published. He and his staff have helped make the road towards publication even simpler and smoother than I could have hoped. I especially appreciate the people who volunteered their precious time to thoughtfully review the draft of the manuscript and generously offer their suggestions on how it could be improved. These include Billy Winn, dean of Columbus historians, who is a constant source of inspiration in my investigation of local history; Dr. David Williams of Valdosta State University, who is, likewise, an authority on Chattahoochee Valley history; Ed Howard of the Cultural Resource Management Program at Fort Benning, who is an absolutely superb editor; Elizabeth Barker, Director of the Historic Columbus Foundation, who is an incredible resource for information about Columbus's architectural heritage; and Clay Williams, Director of Historic Properties with the Mississippi Department of Archives and History, who has been a trusted and candid reviewer of most things I have published.

Numerous others have helped me in the course of my research, including the staffs of the Columbus Public Library,

the Columbus State University Archives, the Auburn University Special Collections Library and Archives, the Mississippi Department of Archives and History, the Alabama Department of Archives and History, Emory University Manuscript, Archives, and Rare Book Library, the Georgia Archives, the Digital Library of Georgia, the Columbus Museum, and the Historic Columbus Foundation. Talented graphic artist Marcolm Tatum created the custom map featured in the driving tour at the end of the book. Aimee Brooks, Registrar at the Columbus Museum, was instrumental in helping secure copies of several historic images. Last, but certainly not least, I thank my wife Tonya and my daughter Zoey for putting up with me spending so much time during evenings and weekends in front of the computer. My sincerest thanks to all of you.

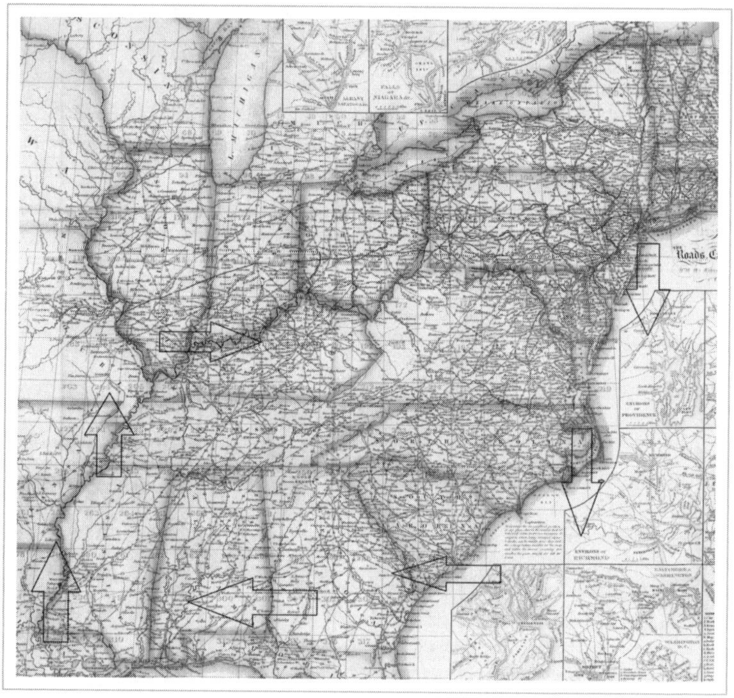

Many antebellum visitors to Columbus were traveling a route known as the "Grand Tour" of the United States, as shown in this detail of the 1842 traveler's guide, produced by H. S. Tanner. *Courtesy of David Rumsey Map Collection.*

→ INTRODUCTION ←

ANTEBELLUM TRAVEL WRITING AND THE AMERICAN SOUTH

Travel narratives were one of the early nineteenth century's most popular literary forms. In an age prior to photographs and in which leisure travel was a luxury very few could afford, travelers who could paint pictures of their experiences with words offered a unique window on the wider world. Readers of travel writers' accounts of visits to distant cities and states valued these accounts not only as entertainment but also as an educational resource that could allow them to become acquainted with people and places most would never have an opportunity to visit.[1]

At the time of Columbus's founding in1828, travel writing was just coming into its own. Hundreds of travel narratives focusing on travelers' adventures in the United States were published in the first half of the nineteenth century, and many went through multiple printings. As always, readers expected travel narratives to be accessible and provide vivid descriptions of the sights, sounds, and manners of distant locales, but with the maturation of travel writing as a defined literary genre came increased expectations that authors would further illuminate life in the places they visited through some form of social commentary. This manifested itself in focused critiques of manners, customs, and traditions as a way to help people better understand the essence of life in a given location. No place in America seemed quite as exotic to outsiders—whether from the United States or abroad—as the South.[2]

Indeed, the South had already become so different from the rest of the nation during Columbus's formative years—due in large part to the institution of slavery—that many already

1830s American stagecoach. *Courtesy of the Library of Congress.*

viewed it as somewhat of a "nation within a nation." While Americans exhibited intrigue with such regional differences, Europeans became positively fascinated by them, penning a large share of the many volumes of descriptions of life in the South written during this era, some of which leaned as much towards sociological analysis as tourist testimony. No trip to, or through, the United States was considered complete without some attempt to deal with the glaring American dichotomy created by the slavery. Hence, a Southern leg of an informal "Grand Tour" became a critical component of seeing America. The tour usually began at one of several locations along the Atlantic seaboard and continued down through Charleston and Savannah before turning inland and venturing cross-country through Georgia and Alabama to Mobile, then continuing on to New Orleans and up the Mississippi before returning east via the Ohio River.[3]

Many of those attempting such a journey would pass right through Columbus, as it occupied a strategic position along major regional roads and had both reasonable accommodations and well-built bridges crossing the Chattahoochee. The city sat at the heart of what many viewed as a wildly exotic province, especially in its first few decades of existence, and provided much fodder for the pages of traveler journals. Here stood a planned city in the heart of the plantation belt, positioned in a scenic setting, yet driven as much by industry as agriculture. Remote yet flourishing, poverty-stricken yet home to many extremely wealthy citizens, diverse yet provincial, ambitious yet backward, and with American Indians wandering the streets to boot, it was the nation writ small.

1

ANTEBELLUM COLUMBUS

It is difficult to appreciate what travelers thought of antebellum Columbus without some knowledge of the community's origins and early development. The city's first two and a half decades—a brief but pivotal era that is the focus of this book—were a period of rapid change that laid the foundation for the future of Columbus. Beginning as a rough frontier settlement, the city rapidly developed into a sophisticated urban center at the heart of a prosperous and growing region. The visitors whose experiences are chronicled here encountered the city at various points in this process and witnessed its coming of age from different vantages. Crucially, the visitors brought with them varying levels of understanding of the city's origins and what future direction it might take. As context for their observations, provided below is a brief chronicle of some of the highlights of the physical and societal growth of Columbus as a nineteenth-century American community.[4]

Columbus was born in an era of dynamic American expansion. By the 1790s, the United States has outgrown and outstripped the lands along the east coast, and the new nation was steadily pushing its borders westward in the first decades of the nineteenth century. Georgia itself represented a microcosm of this national phenomenon, relentlessly acquiring title to Indian lands within its claimed limits after the Revolutionary War in a pattern demonstrating an awareness of the collective sense of manifest destiny that propelled national ambition. By the 1820s, the portion of the remaining Creek domain that lay in west-central Georgia, as well as that of the Cherokees in the northern portion of the state, was all that stood in the way of

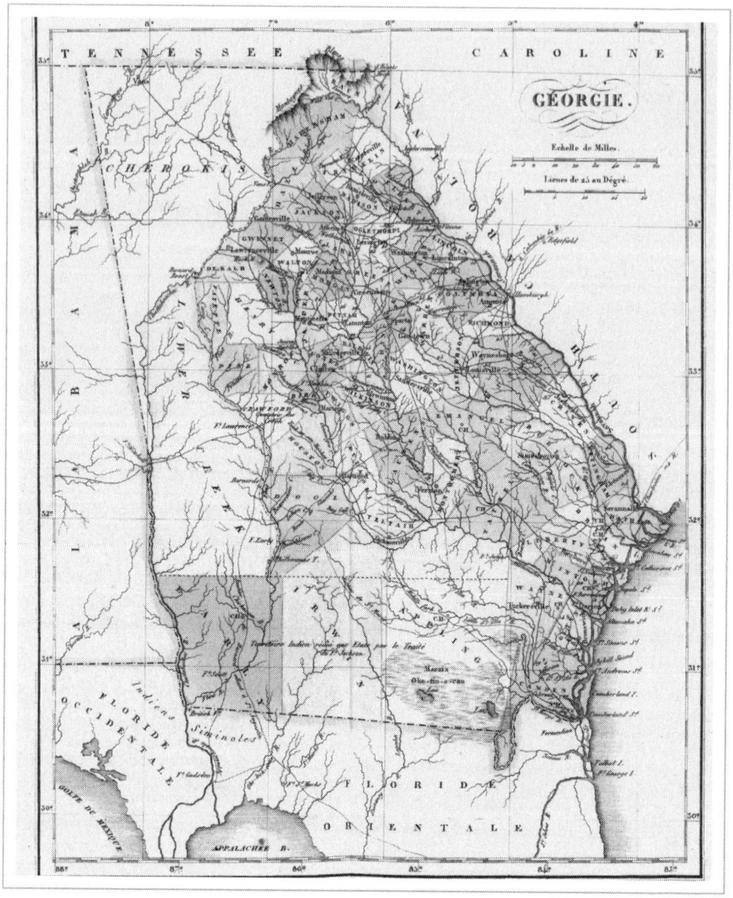

Map of Georgia, 1825, by J. A. C. Buchon, H. C. Carey, and I. Lea, showing what remained of the Creeks' once-expansive domain in the state. *Courtesy of the David Rumsey Map Collection.*

eliminating forever any native title to the state and officially establishing the entirety of its acreage as American territory.[5]

The Creek's land, through which ran the Chattahoochee River, was some of the most desirable for agriculture in a state already animated by the cotton trade, and state leaders determined to have it ceded. Through bribes, threats, manipulation, and fraud, it accomplished just that in the 1825 Treaty of Indian Springs. While legal wrangling over the propriety of the proceedings that led to the compact and its authority would continue for some time, the treaty nonetheless paved the way for the final transfer of the last portion of the Creek's once expansive homeland in Georgia to American control. The ink had barely dried on the document before Georgians and their legislators began planning how to use the land to their best advantage.[6]

Their gaze turned immediately to that portion of the cession adjacent to the falls of the Chattahoochee River. In geological terms, the location is the site where the rocky outcroppings of the Piedmont Plateau encounter the lush rolling meadows of the Gulf Coastal Plain. More practically speaking, the spot marked the head of navigation of the Chattahoochee; from that spot, one had access via water to the Gulf of Mexico, and from there to numerous domestic and international ports. Of more than passing interest was the fact that the rapids at the Coweta Falls, named in reference to the prominent Creek town on the river's western bank, represented a source of an enormous quantity of horsepower that might one day turn the wheels of a variety of industrial enterprises. The legislature wasted no time in carving out this prime location from the larger cession that would soon be opened up to purchase and settlement via lottery. It formed Muscogee County in December 1826 and set aside a five-square-mile section of it for public use. Within that area, the legislature carved out a tract of some 1,200 acres for the laying out of a town to serve as a regional center of trade, which it specified should contain no fewer than five hundred lots.[7]

For reasons frustratingly lost to history, the legislators proclaimed it should be named "Columbus," presumably in reference to explorer Christopher Columbus. To guide the new community into existence, the legislators appointed a group of five commissioners: Ignatius Few, Edwin L. deGraffenreid, James Hallam, Elias Beall, and Philip H. Alston. Distinguished, if not necessarily famous, these men brought to the table their valuable connections and experiences in government, military life, politics, civic organizations, education, religion, and medicine—just the stuff needed for establishing a new city on the frontier. Save for Hallam, who may have already settled in the vicinity, they collectively had very little familiarity with the region, however. Likely all the commissioners knew about the plot of land on which they were to oversee the creation of a city was that it occupied a strategic location on the fringes of what they would have called "civilization," and that it lay covered with a dense forest that would yield itself to their purposes only with the greatest of exertions. At least one of the two assumptions proved to be correct.[8]

Left, Edwin L. deGraffenreid from *Images: A Pictorial History of Columbus, Georgia* by F. Clason Kyle. Right, Ignatius Few from *Images: A Pictorial History of Columbus, Georgia*, by F. Clason Kyle. *Courtesy of Emory University Manuscript, Archives and Rare Book Library.*

The site of Columbus may have been regarded as a wilderness in 1828, but it certainly was not entirely unsettled. American Indians had regularly visited the area for centuries, and the site of two of the largest towns of the powerful Creek Nation, Coweta and Cusseta, lay just a few miles to the south on either side of the Chattahoochee. Smaller outlying settlements stood even closer, and hunters, traders, and fishermen frequently crossed through the plot of land that became Columbus in the years prior to its founding. Such visits apparently grew increasingly common in the decade before the city's establishment, for a small settlement known alternately as "Kennards Tavern" or "Kennard's Ferry" grew up just a stone's throw from the future site of the municipality in the 1820s along the path of the upper branch of the Federal Road. As the name implied, a Scottish-Yuchi trader named Kennard (or possibly Kinnard), operated a tavern and ferry at the site where the road crossed the Chattahoochee. By the time the survey for Columbus began, his tavern had become the center of a small village consisting of a store and several scattered houses of both log and clapboard construction. Just before the founding of

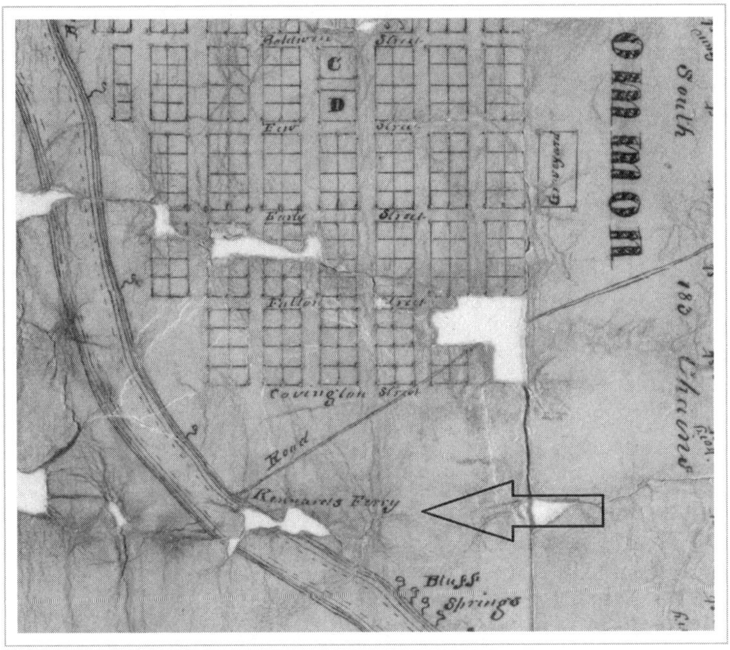

Detail of Coweta Reserve map showing location of Kennard's Ferry. *Courtesy of the Columbus Museum.*

Columbus, the community received a post office with its location recorded as "Wewoka," a Creek word that some believe can be translated as "rumbling water." While not an urban center by any stretch, the settlement's existence had already put the area "on the map," if only for travelers passing through the region, long before the crew charged with surveying Columbus's boundaries arrived to wrest a grid of streets and tidy blocks from the sylvan landscape.[9]

The survey crew quickly found they had their work cut out for them. Although relatively flat and predominantly dry, the site of Columbus lay within a wilderness featuring large groves of hardwoods and pines with several large ponds and swampy areas. Clearing paths for streets and marking out lots began in the dead of a rainy winter, which, while it might have made life relatively more bearable for workmen who otherwise would have been subjected to the blazing southwest Georgia heat and the host of vermin that dwell in the underbrush, still played havoc with the laborers' health. Amidst the rattling of measuring chains, clanging of axes, heaving of cornerstones, and the tedious scribbling of notes, men began to fall victim to the conditions. The son of the surveyor, young Truman Thomas, fell sick, and after a few weeks of illness tragically became the first burial in the city cemetery before the facility could even be fully plotted. The tragedy marred what should have been the crowning achievement for Edward Lloyd Thomas, the minister, surveyor, and late grieving father whose plan for the city created a framework in which it would grow. Work continued with minimal interruption, nevertheless. The time between the first stretching of chain in February to the placing of last corner post was just three months, and lots were ready for sale by July.[10]

Many future Columbusites had arrived long before that sale in anticipation of the auction. The possibility of new beginnings in such a promising locale, coupled with the siren song of the millions of acres of rich soil falling into their laps should the Creek lands on the opposite bank of the Chattahoochee be opened—and this appeared inevitable—drew people from far and wide. A great many of the first settlers of Columbus hailed from central and western Georgia, but others came from elsewhere in the Southeast and even outside of the region. Before the surveyors could finish their work, scores of settlers could be seen loitering about the scarred landscape, housed in makeshift shelters and sizing up the layout of the new town. At least some of them occupied their time by constructing portions of their homes and either stacking the frames in piles or setting them on wheels or sleds, so as to be ready to move to the lots they anticipated winning at auction immediately after the gavel fell. Even Georgia Governor John Forsyth and his staff were on hand for the occasion, the biggest event in the state at the time. The auction began on 10 July 1828 and continued for nearly two frantic weeks. The unimposing window of a simple frame house sheltered by the towering ancient pines and oaks within the town limits served as an ad-hoc auctioneer's lectern. When the dust had settled and the paperwork been placed in order, 488 of the 632 lots available had been sold; those remaining would be purchased soon after.[11]

The first residents of Columbus found a city containing nine streets running north and south parallel to the river and thirteen running east and west. The streets were especially wide at between 99 and 132 feet across, the result of commissioner (and doctor) deGraffenreid's efforts to encourage good health and proper sanitation in the city. Broad Street, designed from the start to be a primary thoroughfare, was even larger—a spacious 164-feet wide. Many of the streets bore the name of noteworthy figures from various walks of life, most of them associated with Georgia: Crawford, Oglethorpe, Troup, Mercer, etc. Others were either straightforwardly descriptive or suggestive of what might be: Short, Front, Broad, Bridge. One street was named after Commissioner Ignatius Few. Surveyor Thomas himself achieved memorialization with a street named in his honor. Though merely stump-filled dirt paths in the summer of 1828, these corridors quickly assumed the look and feel of a real urban center by the fall, when there were an estimated one hundred frame buildings and probably at least as many other assorted structures in the city. Lest one assume municipal sophistication literally came overnight, however, we are reminded that the first ordinance of the young town's government required the removal of all houses still impeding travel on the streets.[12]

Columbus did begin to acquire the trappings of a true city soon enough, though. In May, the inaugural issue of the new city's first newspaper, the *Enquirer*, appeared. It soon began publishing a series of articles chronicling the city's growth. Admittedly often more boosterism than news, the pieces nonetheless served as a barometer for the pace and scale of change taking place along the banks of the Chattahoochee. "Building is carried on in a style that would do honor to our populous cities, and with a rapidity scarcely equaled within our knowledge" raved editor Mirabeau Lamar in an article that appeared early in 1829. "Such is the progressive style, that we frequently find large two-storied houses and well-cleaned gardens ... where but a short time previously we were rambling after game." In the ensuing years, journalists expressed praise and wonder at how rapidly the transformation from "a howling wilderness" to a "flourishing town" had been affected. One local resident, in a less celebratory tone, recalled some of the forgotten inconveniences associated with the rapid pace of settlement, recording that the population grew faster than the capacity to house adequately the new arrivals.[13]

Even relative to its time—an era that witnessed the hurried conversion of wilderness areas into urban trading centers as fast as workers could swing axes and hammers—the development of Columbus proved remarkably swift. Rather than emerging piecemeal through happenstance settlement like so many other communities, the city seemed to burst onto the

Map of Georgia, 1829, by Adel Sherwood, showing the counties carved from the last of the Creek lands in Georgia and the new city of Columbus. *Courtesy of the David Rumsey Map Collection.*

Pont de Columbus, depicting the town, ca. 1830, by Francis de la Porte, Collection of the Columbus Museum, Columbus, Georgia; Museum purchase G. 1983.75. *Courtesy of the Columbus Museum.*

scene as a fully formed urban entity. Shortly after its first birthday, the city could boast of about one thousand inhabitants, and within two years of its founding more than 1,500 people called Columbus home. Before the town could even be found on maps of Georgia, it contained nearly two dozen stores, a dozen attorney's offices, eleven doctors, and several churches. When a gentleman from South Carolina named John Godwin and his highly skilled slave craftsman, Horace King, built the bridge connecting it with cotton-rich Alabama in 1833, the pace of Columbus's ascendancy as a regional hub for trade only quickened.[14]

It follows naturally, then, that one measure of the city's progressive maturation in the antebellum era is quantitative gauging of economic activity at certain points in its development. By the mid-1840s, or approximately a decade and a half following the survey that laid out its streets, the town already contained well over a hundred stores of various kinds, including those specializing in groceries, dry goods, hardware, furniture, clothing, drugs, livery, crockery and tin ware, and books. One tobacconist supplied the needs of smokers, which in all likelihood included a majority of the adult men of the city and not a few of the women. Ten blacksmiths fashioned red-hot iron into an array of tools, parts, and assorted merchandise, much of it likely associated with the community's budding industrial establishment, which included wheelwrights, carriage and gin manufactories, and an iron foundry. A number of hotels, banks, auction houses, and cotton warehouses stood ready to serve both visitors and residents. Many of the city's most visited businesses, though, escaped mention in city directories and official records because they were mobile and not permanent establishments. On any given day in the streets of antebellum Columbus could be found a number of area farmers and bondsmen hawking from carts and makeshift stands their homegrown vegetables, farm-raised chickens and eggs, and freshly caught fish. On the eve of the outbreak of the Civil War, there seemed annually to be more of virtually every type of business establishment, including some that only a few years prior might have been considered luxuries: photographers, ice dealers, and confectioners. Tellingly, there were as many slave depots (three) as newspapers in this growing Deep South commercial hub. Slave traders routinely brought their chattels into town to trade, and auctions were held regularly at multiple establishments, sometimes literally on the courthouse steps.[15]

If you were to stroll through the city, however, you would, of course, have seen far more homes than businesses. Ranging from simple, one-room, log-framed structures to ornate clapboarded mansions in the latest style, Columbus's homes dominated its streetscape. Owing to its being primarily a working-class city, an abundance of basic, one-story frame structures of various levels of sophistication and maintenance were scattered throughout the city. Some featured modest decorative elements that were nods to the classical styles then in vogue in the country's leading urban centers. A smaller number of Columbus's antebellum houses, the domiciles of a growing ultra-wealthy minority, were truly impressive and have been closely recorded in its history, for the exceptional seemingly

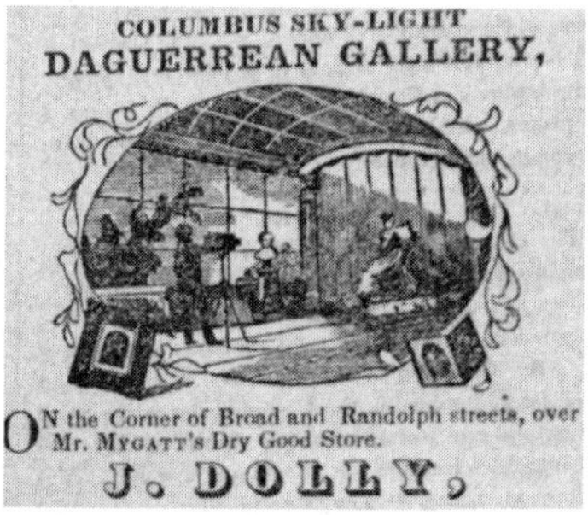

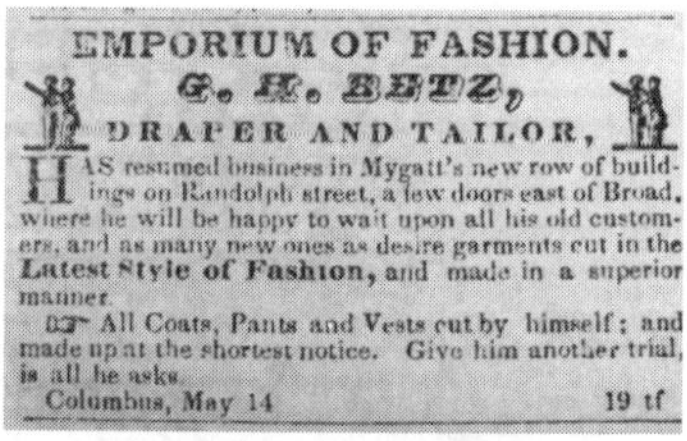

Advertisements for businesses in early Columbus newspapers. *Courtesy of Columbus State University Archives.*

always garners more attention than the ordinary. One street in particular, remembered in local legend as "Golden Row," had an assemblage of several mansions on par with anything that could be found on the more-celebrated plantations in the hinterland. Grand on a timeless scale, these homes showcased the architectural skills of local craftsmen as well as those of national prestige, presenting cutting-edge fashion to passersby and revealing practical, modern, technological innovations to those invited into them for visits. Some of these homes had elaborate and well-tended gardens that burst with color and fragrance almost year-round and provided pockets of sumptuous horticultural splendor in an otherwise fairly raw and unpolished city. A few steps away from most of these urban estates stood a variety of outbuildings such as kitchens, smokehouses, and slave houses. Taken together, they presented an unmistakable, albeit exaggerated, impression of wealth and influence and served as testimony to a sort of arrival of the city's elite.[16]

The establishment of city services and the introduction of urban infrastructural systems demonstrated in other, less ostentatious, ways the young community's coming of age in the antebellum era. The city first elected officers to see to the needs

The Fontaine House. *Courtesy of the Library of Congress.*

The Crawford House. *Courtesy of the Library of Congress.*

of government in January 1829. Officially named a "city" as opposed to a "town" by legislative action in 1836, Columbus held its first mayoral election that year, and at the same time formed its first real city government. That government formed a police force and a "city watch," and created the offices of sexton and health officer. Although an ad-hoc fire-fighting company had existed as early as 1831, the formation of the Columbus Hook and Ladder Company in 1843 marked the beginning of a true fire department—a vital city service in a community filled with closely situated wooden buildings that experienced several devastating fires in the antebellum period. An independent black firefighting company formed in 1854. A reliable source of drinking water and a system for delivering it throughout the city—ironically a chronic problem in riverside Columbus's early years—began to be remedied by the early 1840s by tapping into local springs and installing a network of pipes. The telegraph reached the city in 1848, and gas lights lit up city streets with flickering illumination at nighttime by the early 1850s. Even if the city's streets were notoriously muddy when it rained and dusty when it did not, they at least were clearly marked—a Mr. Pinhorn painted seventy street signs at the rate of one dollar per sign in 1836.[18]

But to really understand early Columbus and the rhythms to which it moved, one must grasp the overarching influence of the river. The very reason for the city's existence, the Chatta-

Left, Mayor John Fontaine. *From* Columbus Georgia, 1828–1978, *by John Lupold.* Right, Second Columbus Courthouse. *Courtesy of Columbus State University Archives.*[17]

hoochee served as a vital trade corridor and important transportation route that imbued its picturesque banks with economic vitality. Although adventurers had discovered gold along the riverbank in 1830, briefly giving rise to misplaced hopes of finding fortunes in river-borne flakes, it was "white gold"—cotton—that became the area's real lifeblood and propelled the region's burgeoning antebellum economy. The community heralded the first bale annually sent downriver to the Chattahoochee's gulf outlet at Apalachicola (the river is known as the Apalachicola River below its confluence with the Flint at the Florida boundary) as a signal event and reported the shipment faithfully in the local papers as the unofficial opening of the busy trading season.[19]

From miles around in all directions throughout the fall and into the spring, the steady clip-clop of hooves announced the arrival of a stream of wagonloads of the Southern staple. Yeoman farmers, overseers, and slaves piloted these vehicles, anxious to see what price a season's work would fetch. Many of these people were making a rare visit into the largest town in the region and consequently prepared to shop in its well-stocked stores to load up on provisions sufficient to last until the next trip. Cloth, blankets, groceries, farm implements, tools, and guns flew off the shelves in a furious spurt of activity. Many paid to have their cotton stored in the city's vast warehouses until it could be graded, sold, and shipped. By 1840 local warehouses were handling nearly 50,000 bales annually, and by 1850 that figure had nearly doubled. As the city's streets seasonally filled with people and cotton lint, a number of locally

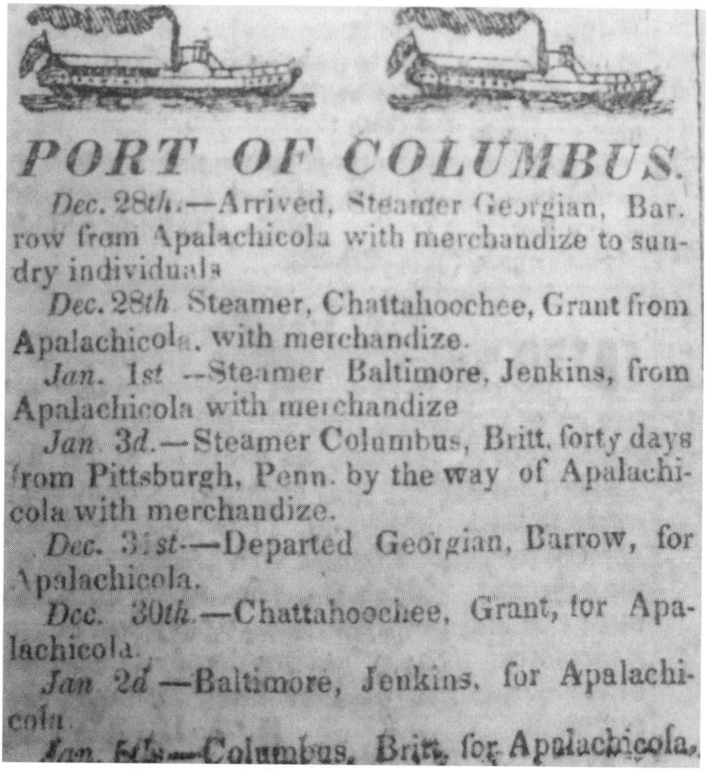

PORT OF COLUMBUS.

Dec. 28th.—Arrived, Steamer Georgian, Barrow from Apalachicola with merchandize to sundry individuals

Dec. 28th Steamer, Chattahoochee, Grant from Apalachicola. with merchandize.

Jan. 1st --Steamer Baltimore, Jenkins, from Apalachicola with merchandize

Jan 3d.—Steamer Columbus, Britt, forty days from Pittsburgh, Penn. by the way of Apalachicola with merchandize.

Dec. 31st.—Departed Georgian, Barrow, for Apalachicola.

Dec. 30th.—Chattahoochee, Grant, for Apalachicola.

Jan 2d—Baltimore, Jenkins, for Apalachicola.

Jan. 5th—Columbus, Britt, for Apalachicola.

Notice of arrival and departure of steamboats at Port of Columbus. *Courtesy of Columbus State University Archives.*

The steamboat *Lowell*, built in 1843 and owned by Columbus businessman Henry T. Hall. From *Images: A Pictorial History of Columbus, Georgia* by F. Clason Kyle. *Courtesy of Historic Columbus Foundation.*

based cotton factors (merchants who worked on commission) swung into action at their desks on behalf of their clients, seeking to sell the crop at the highest price and secure for themselves the greatest profit. Because of Chattahoochee Valley cotton, Apalachicola emerged as one of the South's leading cotton ports, positioned behind only New Orleans and Mobile along the Gulf of Mexico in terms of volume and strategic importance.[20]

All this swarm of activity ebbed and surged with the flow of the Chattahoochee's fickle current. River-borne trade was anything but predictable and far from smooth sailing, as profitable navigation of the Chattahoochee presented substantial difficulties that affected the pace, timing, and scale of economic activity in antebellum Columbus. The river is surprisingly shallow over most of its course from the fall line to the Gulf, and exceptionally so in the frequently dry summers. The fall and spring were usually the best times for shipping, but too much water could be almost as bad as too little—swift currents resulting from seasonal rains made negotiating the river's many sharp turns with the long, cumbersome steamers a tall order and choked the stream with all manner of debris that endangered hulls. High water could also impede steamers, with their tall smokestacks, by making passing under bridges physically impossible. Floods, of which there were some significant enough to be remembered locally with their own nicknames (the "Harrison Freshet" of 1841, occurring just after President William Henry Harrison took office, is an example) could bring all river traffic to a halt for weeks. Even in perfect conditions, however, operating a steamboat could be fraught with dangers from finicky boilers, extremely flammable cargo, and abundant room for pilot error over the river's treacherous course. The average lifespan for boats on the river in regular service was only about four years. Pilots lost dozens of boats in the long stretches of swirling muddy water between Columbus and Apalachicola, their wreckage sometimes serving as navigation hazards themselves. Even if the river ruined lives and fortunes with alarming frequency, most viewed the risk as well worth the reward. It was, after all, for many years the only practical way to get cotton to the international market and the potential for profit enormous.[21]

Those profits so tempted operators that steamboats began visiting the site of Columbus before the town even existed. The

Fannie arrived in January of 1828, and the *Steubenville* a few weeks later. Two others ventured to the new community's rudimentary wharf in the fall, initiating the trade that would come to define much of the economic life of antebellum Columbus. More than a dozen boats operated regularly between Columbus and Apalachicola by 1840, and at least forty served the city in its first quarter century of existence. The boats typically left Columbus laden with cotton and a few passengers, often making stops at some of the nearly two hundred landings between the falls and Apalachicola, where they might pick up more of both. The haunting drone of the whistles announcing their arrival could be heard long before the boats appeared and caused a buzz of conversation and anticipation throughout the city. In a frenzy of shouts and grunts, teams of workmen lifted, tossed, stacked, and carted off the contents of their cargoes to the shops and homes of the city once the boats had docked. The steamboats carried all manner of goods for the growing markets in Columbus, from mundane staples to exotic extravagances: oysters by the barrel, wine by the cask, and furniture by the crate.[22]

In the long run, though, the power of the river to turn the wheels of industry proved more influential than its connection with the Gulf in the course of the city's development. The roar of the rapids crashing over the falls, which can be heard along the riverbank in downtown Columbus today, must have sounded like music to the ears of the young city's pioneering industrialists. Thousands of horsepower are generated by these rapids as the Chattahoochee encounters the fall line—over the course of a little more than two miles the river drops some 125 feet in elevation. All that racing, foaming, clear water beckoned those with the ingenuity to harness its offering. As early as the 1820s, entrepreneurs were already beginning to experiment with means toward that end, and as early as the 1830s local papers touted that the city could become a "Southern Lowell" in reference to the renowned Massachusetts industrial center. Within a few years of the city's founding, a nascent riverfront industrial complex was already taking shape in Columbus, as a grist mill, a cabinet shop, and the city's first textile manufactory each relied on hydropower. Despite its obviously advantageous setting, not until the 1840s did the city proactively encourage industrial activity along the riverfront by selling off the three dozen or so "water lots" along the rapids in the upper part of town that it had successfully petitioned the state for the right to develop. The effort began a transformation wrought by mechanization. It was not so much the number as the scale of the establishments that soon rose along the riverfront that caused the change and led, ultimately, to Columbus's long-standing identity as a "mill town."[23]

While John G. Winter's Variety Mills and the Howard Factory were two of the largest manufacturing concerns to be erected along the rapids, the Eagle Mill proved to be the venture that brought about a sea change in Columbus's workforce environment. Constructed in 1850 by William H. Young, the Eagle Mill soon became one of the largest textile concerns in the South. The plant employed some five hundred people in the mid-1850s, managing production with around ten thousand spindles. The hum of all this vibrating machinery in the Eagle and other factories soon became the auditory backdrop for life in Columbus, the rhythm of shuttles and looms marking simultaneously time and money. By 1860, Columbus had become second only to Richmond, Virginia, in textile production in the South. It also boasted an impressive assortment of other industries, including iron foundries whose pourings of bright orange

Seaborn Jones, former aide-de-camp to Governor George M. Troup, built the first dam on the Chattahoochee at Columbus and the grist mill known as the City Mills. *Courtesy of the Georgia Archives.*

liquid metal lit up interiors in fantastic blazes of light, tinsmithing enterprises whose incessant hammering rang out during the workday, saw mill and cabinetry shops whose constant sawing shuddered the humid city air, and one of the largest paper manufacturing centers in the South just across the river in Alabama. Columbus had definitely lived up to its nickname as the "Lowell of the South" within just a few decades of its founding.[24]

At the same time that all this industrial growth began ushering in a new era in Columbus's history, a revolution in transportation fundamentally altered the city's connection with both the river and the outside world. On 20 May 1853, the city staged a celebration for the recently completed Muscogee Railroad linking the Chattahoochee directly with the Atlantic. More than two hundred visitors from Savannah traveled to town over the route to herald the landmark event. Locals marveled at the remarkable, "fearful," speed of their journey and what it portended. It took their guests a mere thirteen hours, roughly the time it took the sun to travel its arc from the eastern to the western sky, to venture from the far eastern to the far western limits of their state. Efforts toward railroad construction, widely recognized as the wave of the future in transportation even to some degree at the time of Columbus's founding, had begun in earnest in the 1830s. Economic setbacks and a variety of other difficulties delayed the arrival of the rails until the commencement of regular service on the Muscogee line, however. Soon the rumble of steel wheels and the piercing wail of locomotive whistles would reorient the nerve center of Columbus's lively trading network away from the wharf and to the new railroad depot on the east side of town. Steamers would continue to play an important role in the city's economic profile for many more decades, but goods could generally be shipped directly from Columbus cheaper, faster, and more reliably via rail than water from the mid-1850s forward.[25]

But all these facts and statistics are cold without human context. People, not sewers or sidewalks, wharves or factories, are the real heart of any community, and it is in the light of the impact on their lifestyles and aspirations that "progress" is best understood. The population of Columbus grew dramatically during the antebellum period, from about 1,500 in 1830 to about 6,000 in 1850, and approached 10,000 by the time of the Civil War. Relatively heterogeneous, more than half of the pop-

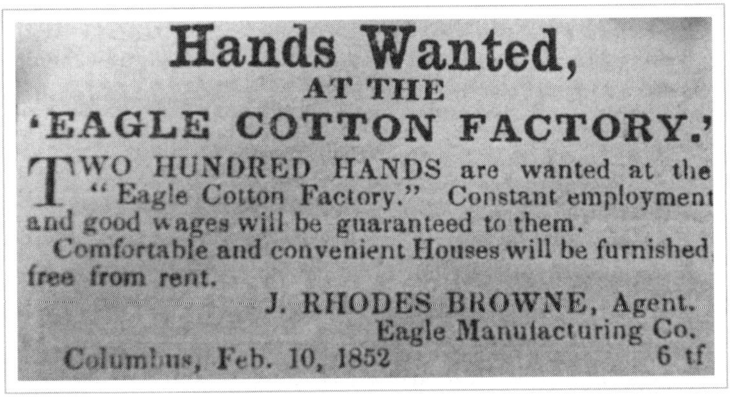

Hands Wanted,
AT THE
'EAGLE COTTON FACTORY.'

TWO HUNDRED HANDS are wanted at the "Eagle Cotton Factory." Constant employment and good wages will be guaranteed to them.

Comfortable and convenient Houses will be furnished free from rent.

J. RHODES BROWNE, Agent.
Eagle Manufacturing Co.

Columbus, Feb. 10, 1852 6 tf

Eagle Manufacturing Company notice of "hands wanted." *Courtesy of Columbus State University Archives.*

Eagle Manufacturing Company. *Courtesy of the Library of Congress.*

ulation as late as 1850 was born outside of the state, and a substantial portion hailed from Europe. Throughout the period, slaves made up about a third of the population, with a smattering of a few dozen free blacks at any given time. It would be this assortment of individuals, thrown together by chance and often having radically different views of the city, its destination, and their role in both, who shaped Columbus into the unique place it became.[26]

While census takers characterized the majority of antebellum Columbus's population as "white" and African Americans played virtually no role in official decisions in the community on any level, it is disingenuous to attempt to explain the early development of the city without giving some consideration to its sizable black population and the influence of their presence on the social life of the community. Admittedly, that consideration is, due to the paucity of firsthand evidence, frustratingly sparse and woefully inadequate to describe their thoughts and feelings with any certainty. The evidence that is available—largely secondhand in the form of laws and regulations, court cases and probate records, newspaper advertisements, written commentary by literate white observers, and even archaeology—clearly reinforces the general supposition that early Columbus society in many ways was actually two entirely different societies yielding totally different experiences and expectations. The stark truth revealed by these sources is that, in general, the white population throughout the prewar era hoped with some rational basis to acquire, accumulate, and ascend, whereas its black neighbors, almost all of whom were enslaved, could look less sanguinely forward to unrewarded labor, unending exploitation, and unrealized dreams. But that antebellum firewall separating privilege and persecution is a major factor in understanding the social milieu in which Columbus emerged, for the two societies can only truly be understood in relation to one another.[27]

Slaves and free blacks may have had little official influence, but they were a constant and conspicuous part of everyday life in early Columbus and contributed heavily to its social grain. It is a difficult truth, but slaves defined the bottom rung of a social hierarchy that white citizens in the city and all across the South believed they would never occupy. Securing forced labor was associated with economic success, and keeping blacks in a subservient position reinforced the self-serving appropriateness of the crude racial lens through which many who guided the region's development viewed the world. No one, visitor or resident, free or slave, could escape the visceral truth that slaves represented, for they were omnipresent in the early city, and their status unquestioned. Bondsmen built the structures in which many white citizens, lived, worked, and worshipped. They labored in many homes as domestic servants and in a variety of businesses, warehouses, and industrial establishments. They congregated with white parishioners in the city's churches on Sundays. They traded, on behalf of masters and

Advertisement for slave dealers Hatcher and McGehee. *Courtesy of Columbus State University Archives*.

even in their own interests, in many of antebellum Columbus's stores. They are listed on police reports and court dockets for attempting to subvert the rules and regulations of a society in which they had no standing. They socialized with those of their race on the streets, and they sometimes formed genuine, if incomprehensible from our vantage point, bonds of friendship and affection with white individuals they invariably called sir or madam and sometimes master or mistress. The city's few free blacks, living on the fringes of society in a middle ground where they were neither bondsmen nor truly free as their white neighbors, were not as numerous but still visible.[28] They were encouraged to keep a low profile so as not to raise awareness of the potential suitability for freedom for all slaves.

There were, nevertheless, respected people of real talent and achievement who came from the ranks of the city's African-American population, such as the celebrated craftsman and bridge-builder Horace King. King managed a remarkable transition from slave to freeman to professional over the course of a lifetime, earning a rare degree of public respect for a man of his race owing to his incredible talent for constructing some of the most important bridges and buildings in the city's early infrastructure. Few African Americans in Columbus, or anywhere else in the antebellum South, were ever afforded the

Horace King, ca. 1850, Collection of the Columbus Museum, Columbus, Georgia; Museum purchase G. 1989.11.18. *Courtesy of the Columbus Museum.*

opportunities with which King was presented, of course. Most toiled in obscurity as they helped create the city and involuntarily gave shape to its values, their individual lives and experiences lost to history and unmentioned in many accounts of the city's life.[29]

If any group had comparable standing to early Columbus's slave population, both socially and legally, it was the Creek Indians. Banished from the portion of their ancestral homeland that lay east of the Chattahoochee shortly before Columbus's founding, they crowded into the last vestige of their once-expansive domain in Alabama in the city's early years. Creek people were a small but noticeable minority on the streets of early Columbus, as dozens of them crossed the river daily from Alabama to work in some of the city's homes and businesses, trade in its stores, and, less nobly, occasionally to drink or beg on its sidewalks. Their imprint on Columbus was unmistakable and intrinsic: they had influenced the clothing and foodways of the area's earliest settlers, hunted and labored alongside them, and even taught games to the children of the new arrivals. But a series of one-sided treaties, destructive wars, proscriptive and discriminatory laws, and organized theft of their lands had left the Creeks desperate and degraded by the 1830s, and it is this unfortunate situation rather than their former independent sophistication that characterized their existence in Columbus's antebellum years. The mere presence of Creek Indians carried symbolic weight that was out of proportion to their numbers. They were a sign that Columbus lay on the frayed edge of a collapsing physical and cultural borderland whose future promised nothing if not change.[30]

It was in an environment of restless, reckless ambition that early Columbus was formed. Many who arrived there viewed it not so much as a destination but as a temporary waypoint towards their becoming—wealthy, famous, powerful, happy. While settlers achieved all that and more on the eastern bank of the Chattahoochee, many set their gaze to the west almost before they had unpacked their trunks and bags following their arrival from "back east." While a sizable portion of Columbus's first residents would come from Europe, a majority hailed from eastern Georgia, the Carolinas, and Virginia. Those established Atlantic seaboard states had been settled by Euro-Americans and their African slaves for centuries, and their soils were becoming worn out from intensive agriculture. In contrast to what they had left behind, the rich, relatively unused lands to which the disadvantaged Creeks tenuously laid claim offered the chance for certain fortune if they could be acquired. The potential scale of that wealth virtually ensured these lands would be the object of theft should the possibility of extricating it from the Creek's grasp present itself. When the opportunity arose, in the form of a host of duplicitous and fraudulent schemes carried out in the name of expediting the terms of the Treaty of Cusseta (1832) and its provisions of de facto removal, Columbus became the unsavory center of a disgraceful scheme of unscrupulous land speculation that opened up eastern Alabama to American settlement and provoked an armed backlash by a faction of the defrauded Creeks.[31]

The Second Creek War (1836–37), as it became known, marked a turning point in the development of the region in

Celebrated locally but vilified and put to death by his own people, Creek Chief William McIntosh, who called the area in which Columbus was founded home, approved the controversial Treaty of Indian Springs that ultimately paved the way for the cession of the last Creek lands in Georgia. *Courtesy of the Alabama Department of Archives and History.*

which Columbus lay and launched it into its ascendancy. Portrayed by panicked locals at the time as a bloodthirsty uprising by the entirety of the remaining Creek Nation, the conflict was, in actuality, a desperate outburst by a faction of the divided and downtrodden natives that resulted in a running series of skirmishes between small bands of overmatched Indians and federal troops and militia supported by allied Creek forces. Nonetheless white settlers and their slaves were driven temporarily into the city—a place of perceived refuge—and national attention was focused on both the city and wider region. Two battles were ultimately being waged as the gunshots rang out: the immediate one an almost foregone denouement to the long tragic drama of the Creeks that brought about their final expulsion and the official cession to Americans of the last shreds of their once-expansive domain, and the other a rekindling of the fiery contest of wills over the issue of where states' rights ended and federal jurisdiction began. That argument had first threatened to immolate the foundations of the national government a decade earlier over the cession of the land on which Columbus lay. When the smoke cleared in the 1830s, residents of Columbus and its environs told themselves that they and those of like mind had rallied together to eliminate the Indian presence that they believed impeded their expansion in both a physical and economic sense and strike a blow for the rights of the states to determine what happened within their borders. They, and the newly formed militia units in town such as the Columbus Guards that had been called out for the crisis, were fully prepared to continue to fight any similar political interference in their future plans from any quarter, including from Washington.[32]

With the exception of the sudden jolt of a national economic downturn in the late 1830s, an era of explosive growth for Columbus and its service area began once the Creeks left. Within a decade, the city began in earnest the journey from a place in possession of enviable opportunities to one that capitalized on them. Part and parcel of this coming of age was a guiding political philosophy first given utterance in the acrimony over the compact that led to its founding and then given tangible form during the Indian war that opened its western hinterland—the people of Columbus vehemently believed in the right of the states to administer their own affairs. A states' rights auxiliary association formed in the city as early as 1832,

General Winfield Scott made Columbus his headquarters when he was sent to the Chattahoochee Valley in charge of US troops organized to deal with the Creek rebellion that became known as the Second Creek War. *Courtesy of Library of Congress.*

and soon a belief in the maxim of self-determination became the litmus test for vetting local leaders. Concomitantly, the rapid transformation of the area in which Columbus lay from an American Indian domain to a cotton empire in little more than a decade gave urgency to the instinct to protect and preserve the institution upon which all the newfound prosperity lay: chattel slavery. Just as Columbus appeared to be coming into its own, the first tremors of the armageddon of nineteenth-century political discourse—the battle over the future of the institution of slavery—could be felt on the banks of the Chattahoochee. Locals rushed to the defense of the "peculiar institution" when it appeared threatened with the same gusto applied to Creek Removal, and then some.[33]

Born of a Creek mother and a Scottish father, Paddy Carr was a frequent sight on the streets of antebellum Columbus. During the Second Creek War, he fought alongside American forces against his rebel kinsman. *Courtesy of Library of Congress.*

Since Columbus had been born out of an impulse for westward expansion, the opening of former Indian lands in Alabama and Mississippi within its first decade of existence had only continued the larger, region-wide migration that served as the catalyst for its creation. When the possibility of the acquisition of Texas by the United States appeared as tensions with Mexico mounted in the 1840s, another wave of westward movement that would swell the boundaries of the cotton kingdom became all but certain. A handful of early arrivals in Columbus had already made it that far west. Former resident James W. Fannin, Jr., led Georgia troops in the Revolution of 1835–36, and, most notably, Mirabeau Lamar settled there in

Mirabeau Lamar. From *Reminiscences of Famous Georgians: Embracing Episodes and Incidents in the Lives of the Great Men of the State* by Lucian Lamar Knight.

time to participate in the fight for Texas Independence, becoming the second president of the new Republic of Texas. Knowledge of Lamar's Columbus connections may have helped fuel the fires of hawkish sentiment in western Georgia as the nation lurched toward a territorial war with Mexico in the 1840s, but the usual mix of patriotism and opportunity largely carried the blame. In Columbus, those who had somehow avoided the lure of moving west already gathered to proclaim resolutions in favor of the acquisition of Texas and vowed willingness to do their part. Ultimately, the city sent some three companies of troops to the Mexican War, making good on the promise to fight for the expansion of both America and slavery, which seemed increasingly to pervade public discourse in

Columbus and across the South as a whole. Future events would only fan the flames of that fervor.[34]

By the 1850s, slavery had become so enmeshed in Columbus's development that separating the two seemed impossible. As the decade wore on and fissures grew between the Northern and Southern states over questions of the role domestic servitude should play in a republican society founded on the noble ideals of liberty, champions of the status quo rose in Columbus to speak in defense of the only way of life they had known. Men such as Martin J. Crawford, James Bethune, Henry L. Benning, and Walter, Alfred, and Peyton Colquitt put the city on the map as a bulwark of secessionist thought with fiery oratory, scorching pens, and aggressive posture. Ominously, their vitriol promised sure and swift retaliation should the federal government make moves that threatened the social and economic structure in which they and those of like mind across the South operated. They at the same time began to advocate for Southern Independence as a viable remedy to their ongoing quarrels with those who might question or seek to limit slavery. A less-outspoken but equally committed sizable minority of businessmen and others who valued as paramount the security of union and predictable order, if not necessarily the liberal idealism of racial equality, somewhat countered the fiery secessionists in the press and the polls for a while. Regardless of significant reservations over the consequences of bombast and the jaundiced eye through which debate and compromise increasingly were viewed, a militaristic voice of righteous self-determination carried the day in the last years of Columbus's final antebellum decade. Its tone and tenor only grew sharper and louder as the nation approached the breech.[35]

Perhaps all this passionate, even indignant, pursuit of fame, fortune, and autonomy explains in part why antebellum Columbus was such a violent place. The city emerged during an era in which affairs involving personal honor routinely ended in physical confrontations. Maybe the rough and tumble nature of a frontier city with a diverse, and in large part transient, population bears the blame; it is easy to forget when reading about the marks of progress apparent in early Columbus that the city remained literally and figuratively in Georgia's "wild west" by the standards of the day. It was, in fact, just a stone's throw from what most at the time regarded as the real McCoy in the form of an Alabama village popularly known as "Sodom." (In truth if Girard, forerunner of modern Phenix City, deserved the appellation, Columbus may have merited the associated sobriquet of "Gomorrah.") Whatever the reason, a sampling of obituaries from the city's early years leaves one with the impression that locals resorted to knives and guns to settle altercations with a discomfiting frequency that bespoke a temperamental nature. Fights in the streets and saloons were common in the rowdy young city, and the matter-of-fact accounts of their occurrence give understated texture to the ragged fringes of pride and temper on which a portion of those that made their home there lived.[36]

"On Sunday morning about three or four o'clock one of those frequent shooting cases came off in a bar room . . . one of the parties got killed instantly," casually noted one resident in his diary. "Joseph Updegraff was on the 17th of April, run through the body with a sword cane, by Britton McCullers, and died a few days afterwards," proclaimed the headline of a Columbus broadsheet shortly afterward. A few days later the typesetter of the same paper set his die to note that "Charnot Newberry was killed by Lewis Jernigan, in a difficulty between them at the corner of Oglethorpe and Franklin Streets . . . Pistols were used." Lest one assume that such affrays were contained solely to back alleys, encounters such as the scandalous murder of Colonel Burton Hepburn by bank president General Daniel McDougald—in the director's room of the establishment—also made headlines.[37]

Maybe that last skirmish had less to do with old-fashioned backwoods brawling than the supposedly more sophisticated "affairs of honor" among gentlemen of standing. If so, it appears to have come across as no more exceptional than a knife fight in a Broad Street bar to readers, for ranking members of early Columbus society participated in their fair share of duels. For the most part, these testosterone-fueled matches of vainglory took place across the Chattahoochee in Alabama for purposes of jurisdiction of authority or the relative lack thereof. In two of the more famous episodes, prominent political figure and future governor George W. Crawford settled a spat with Congressman Thomas E. Burnside near Fort Mitchell in 1828, and later a gentleman named Joseph Camp killed state militia general Sowell Woolfolk in a confrontation in the same vicinity in 1832. Even one of Columbus's mayors (technically termed an "intendant" prior to official incorporation) died from a rival's bullet fired in anger at a distance of measured paces.[38]

Of course, there were many more people in early Columbus that succumbed to accidents and disease than violent confrontations. Falls from horses, injuries sustained in assorted workplaces, and drowning in the river ended the lives of more than a few. A panoply of dreaded illnesses, including dysentery, cholera, measles, scarlet fever, yellow fever, typhoid, and a host of others, carried off hundreds. Scores of people died from vaguely described maladies such as "consumption," "brain fever," and, occasionally, plain "old age." Untold numbers of women died during or shortly after childbirth in the city's early years, and, perhaps even more heart-rending, scores of babies died before they reached their first birthday almost as a matter of course owing to the state of medical knowledge and the living conditions of the day. In a span of six months during 1838, for example, the sexton's report listed well over a dozen burials of infants in the city cemetery. Life, in short, was far more precarious in the first half of the nineteenth century than anything we can imagine today. In a developing frontier community like Columbus, it may have been even more so.[39]

Despite the hard reality of everyday life, however, many social and cultural institutions somehow thrived. Collectively, they tempered the city's violent impulses, provided solace, support,

Trinity Episcopal Church, ca. 1850. *Courtesy of Columbus State University Archives.*

and inspiration to its people, and provided an outlet for a pervasive love of learning and general appreciation of beauty. The first of such institutions to be established were churches. Initially meeting in brush arbors or in borrowed space before they could construct their own permanent facilities, Methodist, Baptist, Presbyterian, Episcopalian, and Catholic congregations all established themselves in the city by the 1830s. The city's first Jewish temple, the second-oldest in Georgia, welcomed its congregants in 1854. Slaves worshipped alongside whites in most of these assemblies, comprising as much as half of the total parishioners, but separate black churches serviced by white ministers, such as the First African Baptist Church, existed by the 1840s.[40]

Within these sanctuaries many of the city's most influential people worshipped and, not infrequently, discussed decidedly temporal affairs and planned civic action. Sometimes this outreach took shape as a variety of philanthropic endeavors that gave form to the more noble aspirations to care for both body and soul, such as funding for poorhouses, orphanages, widows, and other forms of private support for the disadvantaged. At other times, the connection between spiritual and earthly concerns melded even more closely. On 15 May 1836, the Rev. Ignatius Few stood in the pulpit at St. Luke Methodist Church when a man interrupted the gathering with the startling news

First Presbyterian Church, ca. 1850. From *A History of the First Presbyterian Church of Columbus, Georgia, During the First 100 Years of Its Existence* by James J. Gilbert.

that Creeks had fired on a steamboat just a few miles south of Columbus and killed the pilot. Few brought the service to an orderly close, did his best to help those assembled keep their wits, and then offered to serve as captain of a hastily formed volunteer company in a matter of minutes. Less dramatically, charitable causes focused on improving the human condition, such as the "Female Benevolent and Education Society for the Poor," the "St. Andrews Society," and local Hibernian and Temperance societies, benefitted substantially from the support of the community's religious institutions. Whether a city such as Columbus, with no fewer than seventeen drinking establishments in the 1840s, stood more in need of the last organization than others is open to debate.[41]

Columbusites created a number of other types of organizations that channeled energies and helped round off the jagged edges of frontier society. Militia units, a significant but often misunderstood component of early community social structure, flourished. As much fraternal in nature and civic in deed as military in purpose, units such as the Frontier Guards, Columbus Volunteers, Columbus Guards, and City Light Guards became fixtures in the young city as much through marching in parades and helping welcome distinguished guests as through their sporadic opportunities at military service. Other organizations were geared more towards intellectual edi-

St. Luke Methodist Church. *Courtesy of Columbus State University Archives.*

fication. The city witnessed the formation of its first circulating library (by subscription) in its first decade of existence—quite a feat for a community in Columbus's situation. Dr. Thomas Hoxey, a prominent figure in many circles in Columbus's early years, organized the "Columbus Lyceum" in 1839. Privately supported civic engagement enterprises designed to improve social and intellectual life, lyceums were then in vogue in established American cities. Having one in Columbus must have been a point of pride if it did any portion of the work others in the country did, such as maintaining libraries, sponsoring lectures, staging performances, facilitating classes, and more. For those whose interest tended more toward reasoned argument than passive exposure, a debating society formed that had its own library as well. While a true public education system would be something for the future, several small, private academies and legislatively chartered schools, in which the city's children learned and some of its most educated citizens taught, began in the Columbus area during the antebellum years.[42]

A love of the arts among much of the local populace manifested itself in Columbus's early years in the form of support for both traveling and homegrown cultural endeavors. Itinerant artists, working on commission by the piece, regularly visited the city in its early years for stays of a few days to a few weeks. The work they produced, in the days before the widespread availability of photography, satisfied the demand for symbols of self-expression, memorialization, and assertion of status as much as any true appreciation of art in its own right, yet demonstrated to a degree a certain value placed on art. Of a less self-indulgent vein, the traveling art displays that frequented the city served as a sort of enlightened popular amusement. Large crowds paid to view an eclectic variety of panoramas, dioramas, and cosmoramas during short stays in town during the antebellum era. Large-scale canvases of famed European locales, historic battles, and purportedly multi-mile-long rolled canvases depicting the course of the Mississippi River and even the night sky entertained Columbus citizens in its first decades, along with prints of recognized masterpieces. Seeking more lasting viewing opportunities, many in Columbus paid the yearly five-dollar dues to become members of the American Art-Union, an organization that desired to support the development and appreciation of American art through distribution of prints of original work by Americans and offering

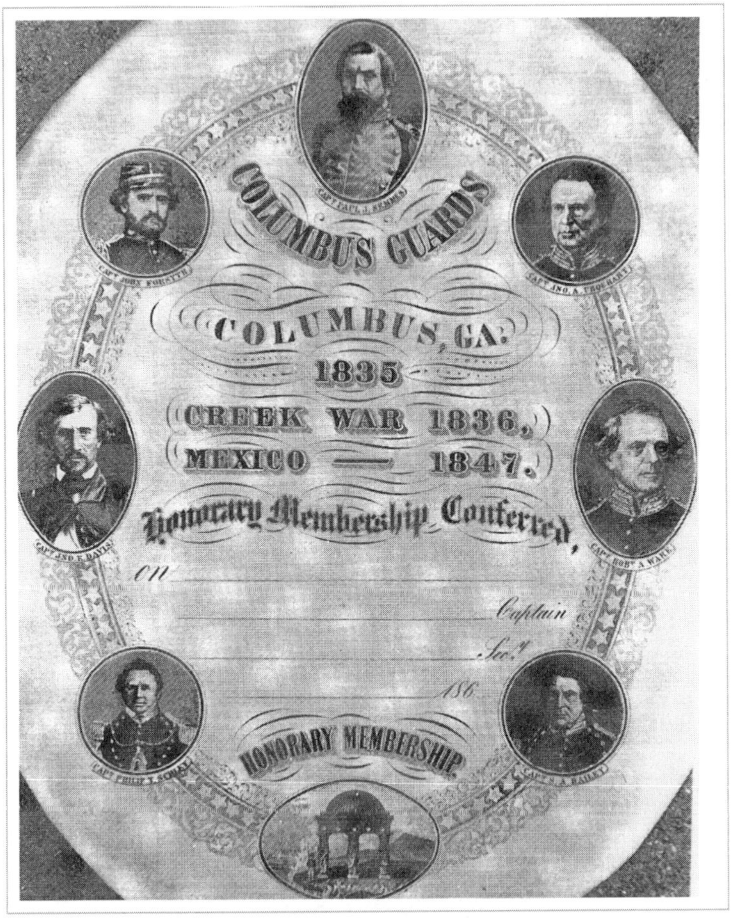

Honorary Membership certificate for the Columbus Guards, heralding the unit's service in the Second Creek War and the Mexican War. From *Images: A Pictorial History of Columbus, Georgia* by F. Clason Kyle.

certain sought-after pieces via a lottery. One local daguerreotypist even sought to emulate the success of the group on the banks of the Chattahoochee by forming the "Columbus Art-Union."[43]

Early Columbus's appreciation of cultural pursuits included a fondness for literature and music. Locals enjoyed reading, and the town had well-stocked bookstores where volumes of classics and the latest in fiction, non-fiction, and poetry could be purchased. A relatively small portion of the city's population had the disposable income to purchase very many books, but those with the means did so enthusiastically. Besides being a

Grigsby Thomas Sr. (above) and *Mary Shivers Thomas* (below) by C. R. Parker, 1838. Collection of the Columbus Museum, Columbus, Georgia; Gift of Dr. William L. Sibley III and his wife, Ruth F. Sibley G. 2005.36.1. *Courtesy of the Columbus Museum.*

prized form of entertainment and education, private libraries communicated a degree of sophistication and worldliness. The town was not without homegrown literary talent, either, as onetime antebellum residents Augusta Jane Evans Wilsom (*St. Elmo*) and Caroline Lee Hentz (*The Planter's Northern Bride*) both achieved prominence as writers. Even *Columbus Ledger* founder, Mirabeau Lamar, garnered fame as somewhat of a bard for his poetry ("Thou Idol of My Soul," "At Evening On the Banks of the Chattahoochee" in *Verse Memorials*), and especially for the memorials to his wife Tabitha who passed away at a young age.[44]

Music proved popular with all classes of people. A steady stream of vocalists from far and wide visited the town in its early years, performing a variety of musicals, operas, and ballads before rapt audiences. Flutists, violinists, glee clubs, and militia bands—the Columbus Guards at one point had its own sixteen-piece marching band—entertained crowds. A surprising number in those crowds could probably play some instrument themselves, as the centerpiece of almost any social gathering seemed to involve someone playing a guitar, banjo, fiddle, or, even more popular, a piano. On any given night, someone strolling through the streets of antebellum Columbus

Left, Augusta Jane Evans Wilson. From *Images: A Pictorial History of Columbus, Georgia* by F. Clason Kyle. *Courtesy of Auburn University Special Collections Library.* Right, Thomas "Blind Tom" Wiggins. *Courtesy of Library of Congress.*

might have heard wafting through the humid air the muffled sounds of tuned strings or voices in rhythm; they invariably would have on Sunday mornings. No local musician, professional or amateur, though, outshone the most unlikely of talents who lived just outside the city limits and who launched his worldwide reputation in Columbus. Born a slave, autistic savant Thomas "Blind Tom" Wiggins demonstrated an uncanny musical ability at an early age that stunned audiences and eventually led to a life of touring both the nation and Europe.[45]

Whether they demonstrated a true local appreciation of a cultural art form or simply a love of one of the oldest types of public entertainment can be debated, but theaters abounded in the antebellum city. Pioneering residents erected a makeshift theater by the middle of the city's first summer, and by 1860 the local populace could take in a show at their choice of no fewer than six establishments. A number of others came and went during this period. In places such as "Temperance Hall" and "Concert Hall," and on occasion in an empty space over a Broad Street store, a variety of traveling dramatic troupes and seasoned actors of renown visited the young urban center and performed the work of Shakespeare and a host of lesser-known plays to adoring crowds. Locals even formed their own drama clubs and theater groups, such as the "Histrionics," providing even more opportunities for Columbus's theater-going citizens.[46]

Other diversions that occupied the free time of those living in early Columbus included circuses, cotillion parties, and masquerade balls. Horse racing may have been the most popular of all, with the track on South Commons becoming the scene of regular gatherings of large, cheering—and financially involved—crowds from all walks of Columbus society. Recreational wagering also took place on less noble contests involving animals, such as cock fighting, which enjoyed a degree of popularity within some circles. There were plenty of other opportunities for entertainment in the city's formative years, as a plethora of visiting amusements such as tightrope artists, ventriloquists, circuses, and even hot air balloons made stops in town. When traveling troupes were unavailable, special occasions provided opportunities for community-wide entertainment. Social events such as weddings provided convenient excuses for revelry, and holiday celebrations such as annual Fourth of July barbecues, observations of George Washington's birthday, and Christmas caroling periodically gave the city a festive air.[47]

The occasional arrival of famous figures from the political world gave rise to impromptu gala gatherings, such as when presidents James K. Polk and Millard Fillmore, or Senator Henry Clay visited the city. Polk's well-documented stopover on the banks of the Chattahoochee—featuring a grand entrance by carriage with band playing, an official welcome by local leading lights, a visit to the home of a prominent area citizen, and grand dinners at a hotel and the city council chambers—reveals the capacity of the young city to "roll out the red carpet" in grand style and throw a party on short notice. The city did not require figures of such national standing to arrive in order to have a politics-centered gala, however, for raucous rallies and debates ranked among the most popular entertainments for citizens throughout the antebellum era. Revivals and camp meetings featuring itinerant preachers proved to be popular events, with the novelty of the affair often as much a draw as the spiritual edification offered. The regular chief amusements of most Columbus citizens were decidedly more down to earth in nature throughout the antebellum period, however. Visiting friends for dinner, a game of cards, some singing and music, or simple conversation, were part of day-to-day life. Discussing cotton and politics on a bench outside of a shaded storefront, knives whittling away on a chunk of wood, occupied countless hours for many.[48]

Due to our awareness of the looming cataclysmic war that would bring a dramatic end to the antebellum era, it is sometimes easy to assume that the people of Columbus were somehow conscious that the foundations of the social structure in which they lived would soon undergo radical upheaval. Such thinking is, of course, flawed, and not just because Columbusites of 1853 could no more predict the rending changes their community would see in a decade's time than those living in the city today can know their own future. Attempting to understand them as somehow mindlessly moving toward an inevitable fate as they discussed politics in their parlors, sweated at their labors in machine shops, shopped in city stores, or lazily fished along the riverbank prevents a true understanding of antebellum society. Antebellum Columbus was comprised of individuals who went about their daily lives consumed by the small circles of self-interest that have driven

Columbus, ca. 1865. *Courtesy of Columbus State University Archives.*

people throughout the ages. Collectively, these singular motivations meshed to create a unique community that on the eve of the Civil War had established its own sense of place on multiple levels. Economically, the city moved to its own already deep-seated rhythms, having carved out a paramount financial niche in a regional trading network whose many seasonal products influenced the ebb and flow of activity on city sidewalks. Culturally, a hard-earned societal infrastructure born of its epoch and situation but also in large part wrought by sheer force of local will gave texture and color to life in the city and went far to smooth its rough frontier edges. Physically, the city's appearance, with its crowded, gas-lit streets, multi-story brick businesses, stylish homes, soaring church steeples, and busy wharf, communicated vibrancy and ascendance even if set against a backdrop of less ostentatious but much more plentiful slapdash construction.

All this urbanity had been forged upon a landscape that a mere three decades earlier had been forest—a dynamic story of a city's becoming played out largely within the simple grid of streets roughly two miles long and a mile wide hewn from nature at its inception, and encountered by visitors at a variety of points in its progress. Their impressions of what they saw follow.

2

EDWARD LLOYD THOMAS'S SURVEY OF COLUMBUS, 1828

The core of downtown Columbus, the very heart of the community and the section of the city that has played, and continues to play, such an important part in defining a local sense of place and lending the venerable old river town part of its unique ambience, would be strangely familiar to the man who laid it out nearly two centuries ago if he were able to see it today. Even though all the landmarks of his days here in the winter and spring of 1828 are long gone, Columbus town planner Edward Lloyd Thomas would be able to navigate the city he quite literally carved from the wilderness with relative ease owing to the integrity of the street plan he so assiduously developed. Through the succession of buildings that have occupied the blocks over the years, the plan Thomas surveyed remains. The grid-like pattern is, admittedly, rather simple and utilitarian, but deceptively important when the story of its creation is considered. It was envisioned by its creator, and brought into being through months of toil featuring both brute force and exacting precision. Columbus's layout is a living monument to a man, an era, and an aspiration, providing the framework on which a community would be built

Edward Lloyd Thomas, moved to Georgia from Virginia with his family nearly four decades before his work along the banks of the Chattahoochee. In some ways his professional career seems in hindsight foreordained, for both his grandfather and uncle were surveyors, and he learned much from his uncle especially. He also trained to become a Methodist minister, however, combining both higher and practical callings that guaranteed steady employment in a frontier state. By the time

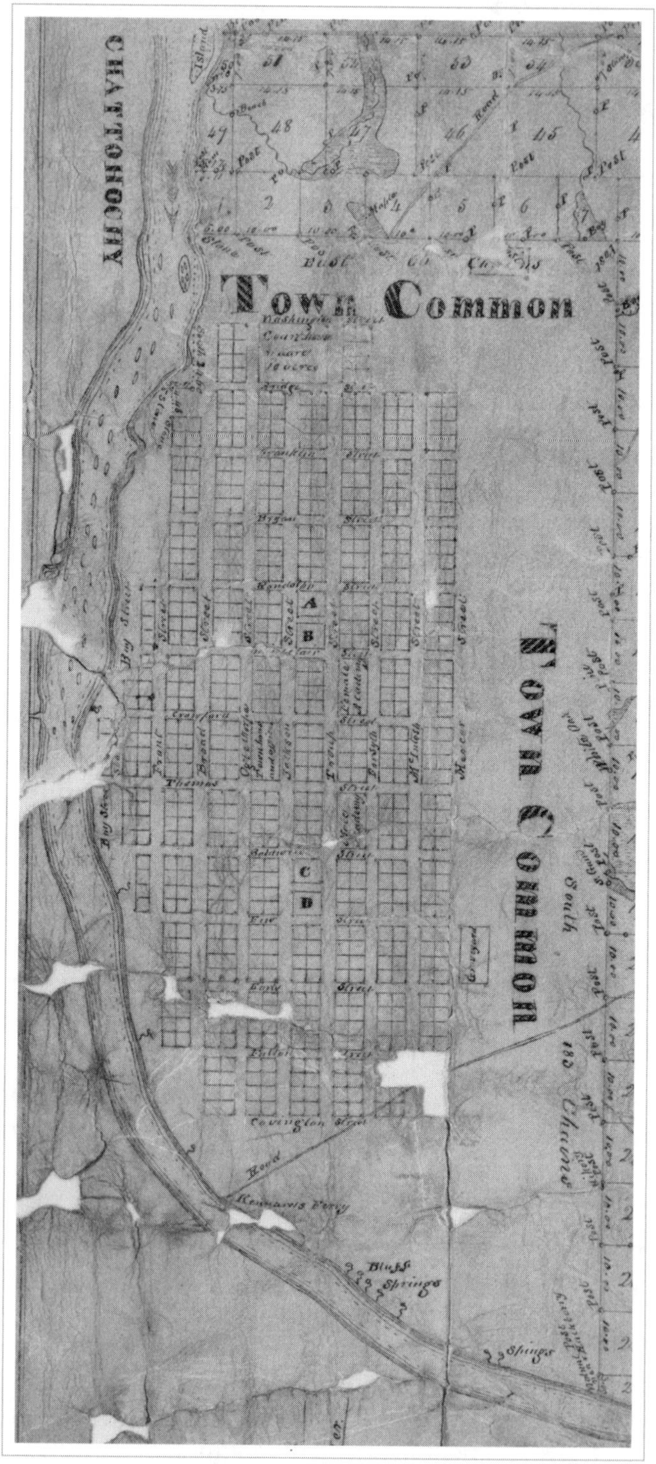

Town Plan of Columbus. *Courtesy of the Columbus Museum.*

Edward Lloyd Thomas. From *Images: A Pictorial History of Columbus, Georgia* by F. Clason Kyle.

of his call to duty along Georgia's western border, Thomas had at least as much experience marking boundaries—between Alabama and Georgia, Georgia and Florida, the Creeks and the Cherokees—as preaching sermons, but precious little in the way of planning towns. Despite this, a sufficient number of those with influence in Georgia's capital, Milledgeville, thought highly enough of his survey work that they tapped Thomas to lay out the legislatively authorized town of Columbus on 16 January 1828.[49]

Thomas wasted no time in getting to work. After a quick trip to Athens to collect his instruments, he "proceeded forthwith to the Falls where I arrived the 27th and on Monday the 28th January entered upon the duties of my office." The "office" in which Thomas would carry out his assignment was about as far removed from government facilities as one could find in 1820s Georgia, for the city that he was charged with planning had to be wrestled from a wilderness on the extreme western border of the state. His notes reveal in graphic detail the scene in which Columbus's creation played out; trees marked the boundaries of blocks and streets terminated or began at rocks along the riverbank. The survey of the "Coweta Reserve," the tract of land on which the city of Columbus was to be located, actually began in deceptively simple style at a long-lost birch tree "being on the Northwest corner on a sluice of the Chattahoochee River." Thomas's notes are replete with references to a variety of indigenous trees as waypoints in the survey—a decidedly rural beginning for an urban community.[50]

Thomas had many preparations to make before the work could begin. "This day our axe-men and chain bearers were engaged making axe-helves & c.," he noted on the first day of official work on the survey. The men soon set to work chopping posts that would be used to mark the corners of town lots. Thomas then employed his crew in obtaining rocks to use as markers for the corners of blocks and the various lots of the future city while he took Columbus's commissioners, just arrived on the scene, to see the site. A few settlers, seeking to get a jump on things, were already milling about, observing the happenings and beginning to construct the rude cabins that would form much the housing stock of the young city. As the commissioners plodded along through the tract, steadily crunching fallen leaves and startling the occasional squirrel, which shuffled up a tree and barked at their intrusion, their journey would have featured periodic stops, during which Thomas pointed out what would be. Though confident, their minds' eye must have strained to see the urban portrait he painted.[51]

On Wednesday, January 30, Thomas and his crew finally began to survey the Coweta Reserve. One of the "chain bearers," charged with carrying the devices by which acreage, streets, and lots were to be carefully measured and laid off, was his son, Jacob H. "Truman" Thomas. Traversing through and over clearings, swamps, fallen logs, and a variety of obstacles, the young man would come to play an intimate, if ultimately tragic, role in the birth of the town. All that lay in the future during the first days of chopping, measuring, and note-taking on a winter's day in western Georgia, however.[52]

Thomas's notes give only hints of the grueling nature of the work he and his small crew labored at from January to April 1828. Commencing his work at a "stone corner" that "represented the beginning point of the line forming the northern boundary of the Town lots," Thomas and his men plunged into their work six days a week. The notes from the survey are not, for the most part, especially revealing. Most are simple entries such as that of Thursday, February 7: "East 1.00 in said line and thence commence line of Bay Street and run South—we run this line about half way."[53]

If there is a day to which Columbus can most accurately trace its physical birth, it is Saturday, 9 February 1828. At the conclusion of that day's work, Thomas noted in his journal: "Finished the plan of Columbus." He sent a copy of the document to the governor for review shortly after, and had copies made to send to officials in Augusta, Athens, and Macon. Such was the nature of travel and transportation at the time that the steamboat *Steubenville,* the first to dock at the city, carried them all on its voyage to the Gulf for them to be taken first to Pensacola and from thence aboard an ocean-going ship around the Florida peninsula before delivery on the Georgia coast. The formal survey of the city, according to the plan, began on 11 February

1828 with the names of "Bay, Broad, Oglethorpe, Jackson, Troup, Forsyth, and McIntosh" given "to so many streets."[54]

Tedium and monotony marked the ensuing days of toil. Slowed by rain, cold weather, and countless obstructions, Thomas and his men ground out streets, blocks, and lots like so many checks on a lengthy to-do list: "From corner on north side of Thomas Street and West side of Broad Street run East 2 c 50 l across Broad St. and thence run North 61 c 26 l to upper end of town lots and return to Thomas Street and run South 52 c 30 l links to lower end of town lots at the intersection of eastern line of Broad Street with north line of Covington Street. Many obstructions in the way." It should be noted that trees were not the only "obstructions" impeding progress. As more and more settlers rushed to the scene hoping to get a jump on choosing the best lots, Thomas noted towards the end of the survey that he had become frequently "much difficulted in passing through houses in running our lines." These cabins were beginning to pop up here and there even before the survey crew could finish the outlines of the new city.[55]

Illness stalked the survey crew, who daily labored in the cool, damp Georgia winter and early spring air. Periodically, some of the hands became sick to the point of being temporarily incapacitated. In late February, Thomas's son Truman became "very sick." Soon, the surveyor's notes were filled with notations on his failing health, an open window to the distraction in a father's heart and mind. After a brief rally a week or so after the first symptoms appeared, Truman took a turn for the worse. His father could only watch helplessly as he deteriorated, keeping his hand to the wheel as he wondered, hoped, and prayed for his deliverance from a malady that he knew might take the boy's life. On March 7, after Thomas finished running the line for Troup Street, he noted ominously "My son Truman *dangerously ill*." Interspersed between notes on his work soon appeared remarks whispering his despair, as he described his son as "very weak and helpless." On Sunday, March 16, members of the survey crew took Truman to the house of one of the area's first permanent white residents. The next day, Thomas sent for his wife. For nine days, Thomas's suffering son continued to "sink and decline under the power of the decease," and at 5:30 in the evening, "precisely one hour after the arrival of his mother," Truman passed away.[56]

Even in the throes of devastating grief, Thomas attempted to keep perspective on his loss. "He is gone and we must go," he noted philosophically shortly after his death. He tried to carry on, his distraction revealed surreptitiously in his logbook by a small typographical error: he wrote that he attended the funeral of his son on Thursday, February 28 instead of March. He resumed work the same day, surveying the "cross lines of streets." Soon the city Thomas carved from the wilderness under a pall of anguish began to take shape. The minutia of detail about the progress of his work in April revealed a gradual healing personally and measuring of progress professionally: "Commenced this evening to plant Posts on corners of lots in blocks situate(d) between Broad and Oglethorpe Streets"; "Planted Posts on corners of lots between Jackson and Troup Street." On April 23, he surveyed lots for churches, and the next day, one for an academy. Every foot of the 10, 440.2 acres in the city survey had been painstakingly planned. There was even a street in the new city, Thomas Street (modern 9th Street), named, appropriately, after its architect.[57]

The grid of lines Thomas cut through the woods along the banks of the Chattahoochee was nothing less than the blueprint for the development of early Columbus. Much of that outline became occupied by homes and businesses in its first decade of existence. Gradually the city outgrew Thomas's plan, expanding steadily over nearly two centuries of development. It is still the beating heart of the city, a tangible connection to the city's birth, a reminder of all those who have occupied Columbus over the generations, and a venerable framework that inherently communicates sense of place.

→ 3 ←

BASIL HALL, 1828

"Every thing indicated hurry"

On an early spring day in 1828, retired British naval captain Basil Hall stood in a small clearing along the eastern bank of the Chattahoochee River and pondered the prospects of the town that allegedly was to be carved from the wilderness around him. Hall, traveling with his wife and child as a sort of professional adventurer, had come to Georgia as part of an extended exploratory journey throughout the United States. During his year and a half trek he planned to observe America's society and landscape and publish an illustrated record of his journal upon his return to England.[58]

Hall listened attentively as his guide boisterously referred to the spot on which he stood—a narrow lane among the pines and oaks marked off by surveyors' stakes—as the very center of the future city. Looking around, he and his companions could eventually discern the series of roughly hewn paths into the woods branching off the main lane that were to become the streets of the town. All around he heard the sound of hammers, axes, and saws, as settlers and speculators began the labor-intensive process of clearing the land. Hall pulled out his camera lucida, a cutting-edge device that functioned as the camera of its day, and prepared to record in visual form the birth of a city. Though somewhat doubtful as to the prospects of survival for this "embryo town," Hall carefully chose the best vantage point from which to record a likeness of this "very curious place." He had seen a good deal more of the world than most men of his day by the time he visited Georgia, and as a result of his experience writing books based on his travels he

Basil Hall's sketch of Columbus, which he titled *Embryo Town.* Collection of the Columbus Museum, Columbus, Georgia; Museum purchase made possible by the Evelyn S. and H. Wayne Patterson Fund G. 2007.14. *Courtesy of the Columbus Museum.*

knew innately how best to represent the tumultuous origin to which he bore witness. As the prism in the camera lucida reflected the scene he beheld in front of him for tracing, Hall carefully began creating the first known view of the city of Columbus.[59]

The finished image Hall produced that day first appeared to the public in *Forty Etchings, Made with the Camera Lucida,* an image-based companion volume to his narrative *Travels in North America,* in 1829.

Hall's image and account of his experience in Columbus have served as invaluable reference sources for generations of people interested in learning about the city's origins. Almost two centuries after their creation, these images remain among the most definitive and compelling accounts of Columbus's birth. What Hall learned about the progress of the city before his death in 1844 is uncertain; in his *Travels* he only wrote that he regretted that he had not heard anything about the development of Columbus since the day of his visit. He surely would have marveled at just how well this "strangely concocted town" developed within a short period of time and to what degree it soon prospered.[60]

We pick up his narrative as he enters the city:

. . . A gentleman—one of the assembled inhabitants—had been kind enough to accompany us from the Agency, to show off the Lions of this singular place. The first thing to which he called our attention, was a long line cut through the coppice-wood of oaks. This, our guide begged us to observe, was to be the principal street; and the brush-wood having been cut away, so as to leave a lane four feet wide, with small stakes driven in at intervals, we could walk along it easily enough. On reaching the middle point, our friend, looking around him, exclaimed, in raptures at the prospect of the future greatness of Columbus—"Here you are in the centre of the city!" In a very short time, he assured us, it would be no longer a mere path, but a street sixty yards wide, and one league in length! By keeping a bright look-out as we proceeded, we could detect other similar cuts into the forest, branching off at right angles to this main avenue—as it was to be called. As yet, however, these cross streets were only indicated by a few stakes driven in by the surveyors.

After threading our way for some time amongst the trees, we came in sight, here and there, of huts made partly of planks, partly of bark, and at last reached the principal cluster of houses, very few of which were above two or three weeks old. These buildings were of all sizes, from a six-feet box or cube, to a house with half-a-dozen windows in front. There were three hotels, the sign belonging to one of which, I could observe, was nailed to a tree still growing untouched in the middle of the street. Another had glazed windows, but the panes of glass were fixed in their places merely for the time, by a little piece of putty at each corner. Every thing indicated hurry. The direction and width alone of the future streets were adhered to, but no other description of regularity could be discovered. As none of the city lots were yet sold, of course no one was sure that the spot upon which he had pitched his house would eventually become his own. Every person, it seemed was at liberty to build where he could find room, it being understood that forty days after the sale would be allowed him to remove his property from the ground on which it stood, should be not himself become its purchaser. In consequence of this understanding, many of the houses were built on trucks—a sort of low, strong wheels, such as cannon are supported by—for the avowed purpose of being hurled away when the land should be sold. At least sixty frames of houses were pointed out to me, lying in piles on the ground, and got up by the carpenters on speculation, ready to answer the call of future purchasers. At some parts of this strange scene, the forest, which hereabouts consists of a mixture of pines and oaks, was growing as densely as ever; and even in the most cleared streets some trees were left standing, I do not well know why. As yet there had been no time to remove the stumps of the felled trees, and many that had been felled were left in their places; so that it was occasionally no easy matter to get along. Anvils were heard ringing away merrily at every corner; while saws, axes, and hammers were seen flashing amongst the woods all round. Stage-coaches, travelling wagons, carts, gigs, the whole family of wheeled vehicles, innumerable, were there. Grocery stores and bakeries were scattered about in great plenty—and over several doors was written, "Attorney at Law."

One of the commissioners, from the State of Georgia, who had the management of this extraordinary experiment in colonization, assured me, there were upwards of nine hundred inhabitants already collected together, though it was expected that four months must still elapse before the sale could take place, or the city have any legal existence! Many of these people, being without houses, or even sheds, were encamped in the forest. Some lived in wagons, and many persons strolled about, to pick up quarters and employment where they best could. As all sort of artificers were in great demand, it was a fine harvest for carpenters and blacksmiths. I was told that, upon a moderate computation, there would probably be assembled, on the day of sale, between three and four thousand people, ready to inhabit the new city. I can well believe this, for, during the short period we were there, many new-comers dropped in from different directions, out of the forest—like birds of prey attracted by the scent of some glorious quarry.

It must have been a curious sight, after the auction, to witness the scatter which took place when the parties came to claim each his own property—to demolish or remove the old, and raise the new dwellings—to say nothing of the entangled machinery of police and other municipal arrangements—the mayor and aldermen to get up,—the town taxes to levy;—the school,—the jail,—the court-house,—the church, all to be erected. In other places, these things rise up by degrees—but here they must have taken their date all at once, and all in a body!

I could form no idea, from what I saw or heard on the spot, how this strangely concocted town would get on...[61]

Chutes de la Chattahoochie by Francis de la Porte. Collection of the Columbus Museum, Columbus, Georgia; Museum purchase G. 1983.74. *Courtesy of the Columbus Museum.*

4

MARGARET HUNTER HALL, 1828

"Inhabitants without a town"

Basil Hall's wife, Margaret Hunter Hall, accompanied the captain on his journey with a young child in tow and later recorded her own account of the family's epic journey in the form of a series of descriptive letters to her sister, Jane. These detailed and insightful letters, a "triumph of effortless observation," according to Una Pope Hennessey, who edited the correspondence for publication in the 1930s, are a remarkable source of information in their own right and provide additional information on the Halls' eventful journey. Margaret's notes on the family's visit to Columbus as the city took shape in late March 1828 come from a letter written at "Columbus at the Falls of the Chattahoochie, Georgia." Her account of a day spent at the site of the future city illuminates her husband's brief notes by providing, with a touch of humor, additional details about the situation the couple encountered:

> Basil says that he has seen a town without inhabitants, but that never before saw inhabitants without a town. To such a place we have got now, as I shall tell you in the course of my narrative.... When the United States purchased the land lying between the Flint and Chattahoochie Rivers from the Creek Indians, they made a lottery of it, dividing into lots 202½ acres each, and every one over age in the state of Georgia had a right to draw. A man with a wife had two draws, or chances, and one with a wife and family had three. But at the same time a certain portion was reserved five miles square for the purpose of erecting a town, and this portion is at the

Falls of the Chattahoochie, a very beautiful situation indeed. The lots of the town consisted, some of an acre, and others of half an acre, and around are some larger bits of ten and twenty acres which will make nice villas. All this you will observe is to be, for as yet the town is a thick forest, with the exception of some temporary wooden buildings erected to shelter the numerous bidders from all parts of the Union who are waiting for the sale of lots which is to commence early in July.

Our companion pointed them out to us as we walked along, for we had an hour's walk from the water side along streets staked out amongst the trees. "And now," he said, as we were on the most rugged beshrubbed part of the path, you are in the heart of the city. The little temporary streets at which we at length arrived presented a very strange appearance, little log and frame houses, most of them intended to be moved to some other situation a few months hence, but in the meantime exhibiting very imposing signs such as T. Gordon, Attorney-at-Law, "Bake House" and so on. Crowds of gentlemen, American gentlemen, remember, in large cloaks and beards of a week's growth lolling about with the forefeet of their chairs in the air according to custom, and some of them showing symptoms that whisky has already found its way to Columbus. Hotel signs swung among the trees, and we were very well accommodated at the principal one. There are several commissioners on the part of the United States Government residing there for the purpose of arranging the sales. To one of these, Dr. de Graffenreid, we had a letter, and he introduced all the others, and a whole host of people besides, to us.

It was four o'clock when we reached Columbus, and after walking down to visit the Falls, or rather Rapids, Basil took advantage of the remaining daylight to make a sketch. This, as usual, brought all the idlers to stare, and he soon had a mob around him. Two long hours passed before there was a morsel ready for us to eat, and we had nothing since ten o'clock, however, at last our supper was ready and having dispatched it we walked off to one of the adjoining houses, for each room was a separate house, to see the plan of the one, and there we sat talking with numerous gentlemen till I got so sleepy that I could sit no longer.[62]

5

THE "MILLEDGEVILLE RECORDER", 1828

"The prospects of this new town are truly flattering"

Nineteenth-century newspapers served as the preeminent information source of their day. In the era before radio, television, and the internet, papers were the only official source for news. When one of the largest newspapers in the state of Georgia, based in Milledgeville, carried a story about the founding of a new city on its western frontier, it received the attention of a wide audience within Georgia and beyond. On 2 August 1828, such an article appeared in the *Milledgeville Recorder*, one of the most widely circulated papers in the Deep South in the era of Columbus's founding. A correspondent from the newspaper visited the young town of Columbus that summer to see firsthand how the planned community was coming along. His dispatch—equal parts description and prognostication—became one of the first, if not *the* first journalistic accounts of the city. The author offered a very complimentary description, to the point of bordering on boosterism. Readers in eastern Georgia and elsewhere in the South certainly read it with great interest, nevertheless. Many of them would soon participate in the rush for the newly opened lands of western Georgia in which Columbus lay and that would fundamentally alter the state's cultural, political, and economic landscape.[64]

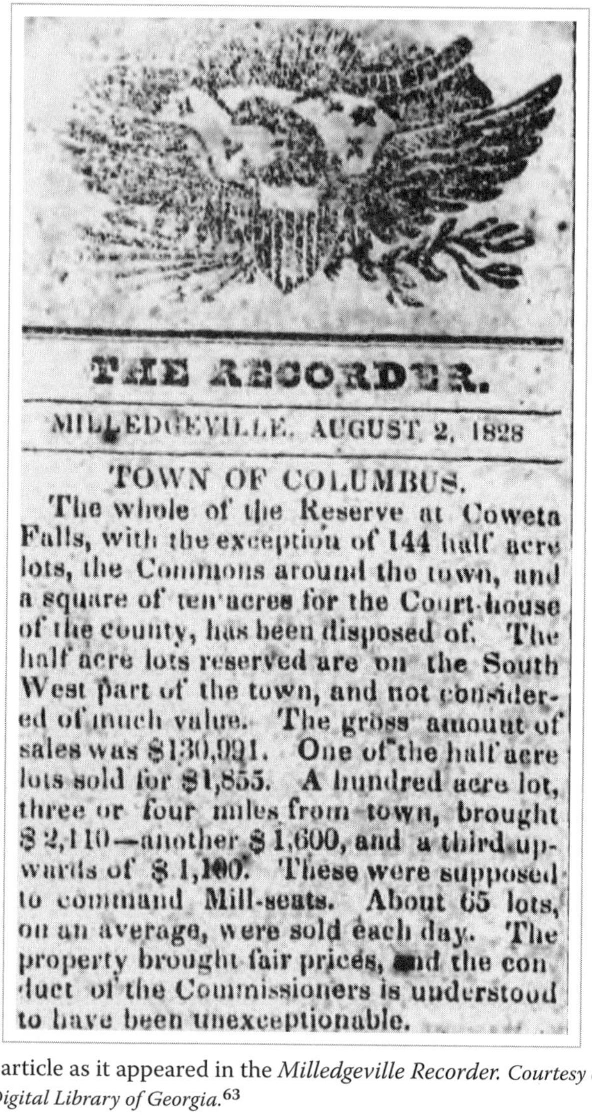

THE RECORDER.

MILLEDGEVILLE, AUGUST 2, 1828

TOWN OF COLUMBUS.

The whole of the Reserve at Coweta Falls, with the exception of 144 half acre lots, the Commons around the town, and a square of ten acres for the Court-house of the county, has been disposed of. The half acre lots reserved are on the South West part of the town, and not considered of much value. The gross amount of sales was $130,991. One of the half acre lots sold for $1,855. A hundred acre lot, three or four miles from town, brought $2,110—another $1,600, and a third upwards of $1,100. These were supposed to command Mill-seats. About 65 lots, on an average, were sold each day. The property brought fair prices, and the conduct of the Commissioners is understood to have been unexceptionable.

The article as it appeared in the *Milledgeville Recorder. Courtesy of the Digital Library of Georgia.*[63]

"The Town of Columbus"

The whole of the Reserve at Coweta Falls, with the exception of 144 half acre lots, the Commons around the town, and a square of ten acres for the Court-house of the county, has been disposed of. The half acre lots reserved are on the South West part of the town, and not considered of much value. The gross amount of sales was $130,991. One of the half acre lots sold for $1,855. A hundred acre lot, three or four miles from town, brought

$2,110—another $1,600, and a third upwards of $1,100. These were supposed to command Mill-seats. About 65 lots, on an average, were sold each day. The property brought fair prices and the conduct of the Commissioners is understood to have been unexceptionable.

The prospects of this new town are truly flattering. One of the Editors of this paper attended the sales, and can speak of its local situation and rare advantages from personal observation. The town is laid off on a high, level, dry plain, immediately opposite to the Falls or rather Rapids of the Chatahoochie, on an elevation of forty or fifty feet above the river. Broad street, which is a mile and a half long and 164 feet wide, appears to be, from one end to the other, a perfect level. The streets running parallel with the river are Front, Broad, Oglethorpe, Jackson, Troup, Forsyth, McIntosh and Mercer, all of which, except Broad street, are 132 feet wide. The cross-streets are Washington, Bridge, Franklin, Bryan, Randolph, St. Clair, Crawford, Thomas, Baldwin, Few, Early, Fulton, and Covington, each of the width of 99 feet.

The town lots are laid off about an equal distance above and below the head of Steam-boat navigation; none of them extend to the river bank, but a beautiful promenade is left along its whole extent, which is the highest ground on the plan of the town, and affords a commanding view of the picturesque rapids above, and of the placid deep river below. At the head of navigation the river is upwards of 100 yards wide and from three to eight feet deep. A few hundred yards above, at the rapids, the usual width of the river is 260 yards—but when we saw it, at an unusual dry time, the whole current of water rushed, with inconceivable velocity, through a single aperture in the rocks of 50 or 60 feet wide. Rock, Trout, Perch and Cat Fish are caught here in abundance—the former weighing as much as 40 pounds, and selling of this size for a dollar and a quarter each. A number of fine springs break out along the river bluff—the water transparent, cool and palatable. From the high bluff you pass on a sandy beach to the rocks which encompass the river—there is no mud and not an acre of low grounds or marsh on either side of the river near the town. The place has every appearance of being healthy, and is decidedly better situated in this respect than Augusta, Milledgeville or Macon. The rapids of the Chathoochie at Coweta Falls very much resemble those of James river at Richmond, Va.

That Columbus will become a very important town, and very soon too, we cannot for a moment doubt. Such was the opinion of all who attended the sales, and many shrewd men from different parts, attracted by curiosity or the prospect of speculation, had congregated there. The population in February last was about 500—it is now said to be upwards of 1300. A number of frame buildings, set on blocks, ready to be moved to any lot, were offered for sale, and found ready purchasers. One gentleman contracted for the erection of buildings, to be put up with all possible expedition, to the amount of $5000. Another advertised for 200,000 brick, for the erection of a brick building. The bricks made at Columbus are of a superior quality, and many of the buildings, when timber becomes more scarce, will probably be made of brick.

Of the facilities which Columbus has for trade we took some pains to inform ourselves. An intelligent gentleman who has been some time engaged in the traffic carried on between that place and New Orleans assured us, that goods could be brought from thence to Columbus in eight days, and that in two years the cost of transportation from the one place to the other would be under half a dollar the hundred weight. Sugar, Molasses, Rum, Salt, Flour, Whiskey, Bacon &c. will consequently be sold in Columbus at a lower price than they can be purchased at any inland town in the State. Sugar, and its offals, Molasses and Rum, will be produced in a year or two on the Chatahoochie itself and the country adjacent to it in great abundance, and will no doubt be sold in Columbus for a fourth or a fifth less than the article of similar quality can be afforded in Milledgeville and Macon. The people of Columbus say they can carry Sugar from their town in wagons to either of those places and make a profit on the article.

The country on which Columbus relies for support is extensive and fertile, composing the counties of Muscogee, Marion, Lee, Harris, Talbot, Upson, Pike, Meriwether, Troup, Coweta, Carroll, Fayette, DeKalb,

Gwinnett, Hall and Habersham; when the Indians are removed, the trade of a large portion of the Cherokee country will certainly go to that town, and also the most valuable portion of the Creek Territory, comprising the fertile lands about Tuckabatchee and the desirable country between the Coosa and Tallapoosa rivers. But one thing can happen to injure the fair prospects of Columbus, and this is the rearing up of a town, at some future day, on the opposite side of the river. Of this there could be but little danger if a free Bridge were established across the Chatahoochie at the Rapids, where nature seems to have designed that one should be built—the cost would not be considerable, and the Legislature of our State will act wisely in turning its attention, at an early period, to this object. The city of Augusta pays into the public treasury upwardly about $22,000, every cent of which would be lost to the State if that emporium of commerce were located on the opposite side of Savannah River. Columbus will in a few years add, by its quote of taxes, greatly to the public treasure of the State, if a rival City do not spring up in its neighborhood on the Alabama side of the river. Having the start, Columbus, favorably situated as it is, can scarcely fail to outstrip any rival, if the safe and free passage of the river be secured.[65]

The facility and expedition with which the Chatahoochie is descended to the Gulf of Mexico is almost incredible. Two persons in a canoe landed at the place of deposit on the Bay of Appalachicola in 48 hours, after leaving Columbus, stopping several times to hunt on their run down the river. It is navigated at present above the Rapids from Hall county to Miller's Bend, thirty miles from the town. At no great expence the navigation for pole boats can be brought, we are assured, within four miles of Columbus. The carriage of produce and goods over this short distance must be effected for a time in wagons on a common rough road, but the time cannot be distant, when a canal or Rail Road over that space will connect more effectually the communication between the upper and lower sections of this majestic river.

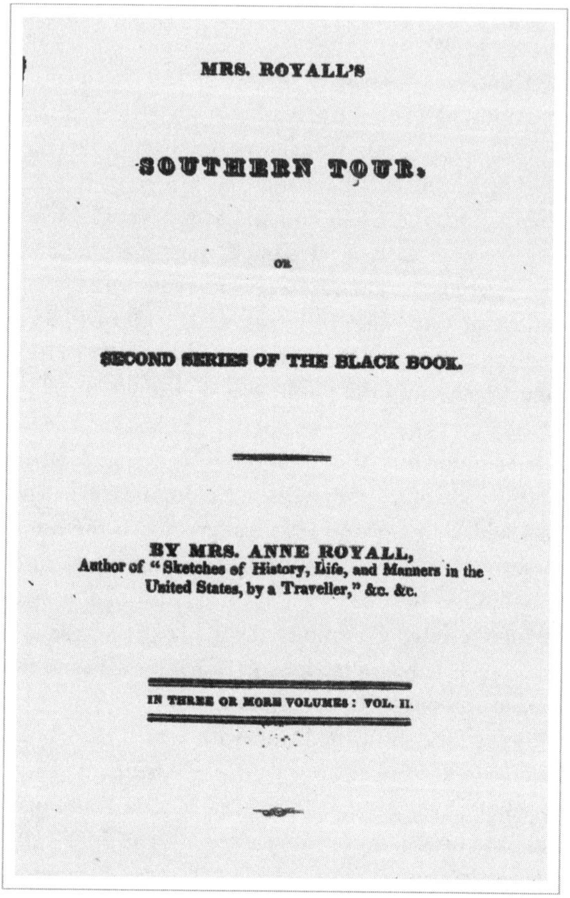

MRS. ROYALL'S

SOUTHERN TOUR,

OR

SECOND SERIES OF THE BLACK BOOK.

BY MRS. ANNE ROYALL,
Author of "Sketches of History, Life, and Manners in the United States, by a Traveller," &c. &c.

IN THREE OR MORE VOLUMES: VOL. II.

From *Mrs. Royall's Southern Tour or Second Series of the Black Book.*

6

ANNE ROYALL, 1830

"This is to be the Savannah of the west!"

Anne Royall's account of her 1830 visit to Columbus describes a relatively sophisticated and urbane community for a place that was only two years old. The town's well-established appearance astonished Royall, who, although a knowledgeable and experienced traveler, professed to have not even heard of Columbus before arriving as close by as Macon. The lush and verdant nature of the Chattahoochee Valley drew her attention and comment, as did the dignity and gentlemanly qualities of many of those she met in her brief stay; some of these people were already recognized as local luminaries and their names figure prominently in local history.[66]

Royall seemed genuinely to like Columbus, in no small part because the city received her in style. The fact that residents regarded her as somewhat of a celebrity is, in itself, one measure of the frontier town's worldliness. An emerging travel writer who had published her first major work after an extended trip through Alabama only a few years prior her visit to Columbus, Royall's reputation as an outspoken, opinionated, and candid *female* observer of American society made her a novel and polarizing figure in the nation's literary scene. Royall, after all, supposedly conducted an uninvited grilling of President John Quincy Adams as he bathed to demand she receive a pension for the military service of her deceased husband after originally having the request denied. There is some truth to the claim by many that Royall was the first professional female journalist in America. Hints of her unusual watchfulness regarding the propriety of governmental operations can be found below, as well as a glimpse of early Columbus society and its reaction to a visit from a minor celebrity who most likely was recognized only by informed readers:[67]

> The land now, is generally rich, but thinly settled, the country being quite new, and passing through the land lying between the Oakmulgee and Chattahoochie: we crossed some piney hills, and dined at Knoxville, called after friend Knox . . .
>
> About 12 o'clock, under a burning sun we reached Columbus, another, and for the same time, a still more flourishing town than Macon, and has far greater advantages, being on the Chattahoochie, (pronounce it who can) a large beautiful stream, navigable for steam-boats to this place. This is to be the Savannah of the west! And they are pushing their capital here as at Macon. Astonishing! What a fertile State this is—and emphatically canaled with rivers, no wonder they oppose internal improvement. This is the best land I have seen, since I left Tennessee River, eight years since! It is impossible for land to be richer. The great walnut trees, grape-vine, and other monstrous growth! I thought no more of flowers!
>
> It is surprising, that the poor and indigent, the man who works daily for his bread, in the old worn-out States, does not come and settle upon land, where he would, at least, be paid for his labor.
>
> Nothing is stationary, where the land is rich—no man can be poor, and want is unknown. Columbus leaves Macon far behind in rapidity of growth.
>
> It contains 2 Churches, 1 Bank, 18 Stores, 11 Doctors, 12 Lawyers, 1200 inhabitants, and only TWO years old!!! I never heard of Columbus, till I came to Macon, from which it is distant, nearly 100 miles, south west. One of the richest spots on the globe. Without the handsome scenery, however, of Macon, the falls near this, on the Chattahoochie are 300 feet: I was really so much overcome by the heat, that I did not visit the falls, I had a scheme in my head, too, which, if I succeed, would leave me no time—the scheme was to go as far as Fort Mitchell that evening.
>
> The mail stops here again from the time we arrived till next morning 9 o'clock! What all this means I should

like to know. The United States' mail ought not to stop, day nor night, till it arrives at New Orleans, where it is all important it should arrive as soon as possible. My plan, therefore, was, as the post-master, I understood, was the son of my friend Gov. Van Ness, (our minister,) to get him to close the mail that evening, and coax up the driver to go on to Fort Mitchell, where I could see how matters went on there, and pursue my journey to Montgomery in this stage. Otherwise, if I stopped at all at Fort Mitchell, I must await the next stage, two days. I should have been pleased to have spent a week at Columbus, but I had yet a long way to travel to New Orleans, and the heat was even now very oppressive. I sent for Mr. Van Ness, and soon brought him over and the driver, but the insolent ruffian would not agree to it.

At length, however, Mr. Van Ness agreed to take me to the Fort that evening in a private carriage, so, through this gentleman's politeness, I carried my point. This being settled, I took some refreshments and received my friends. Columbus is the only town I ever visited in my life that might be said to contain no rabble, and though my time was short there, not more than 3 to 4 hours, I never left a place under stronger impressions of esteem and friendship. After seeing the principal gentlemen of the place in a small upper room, being told there were a great many down stairs who were anxious (but were afraid to come up stairs) to see me, I went down to a large parlor. The parlor soon filled, and even the back and front yards were covered with people of all ranks and ages. But never did I see a collection before nor since that behaved with more decorum. They were as still as midnight: not a smile, not a word, not a whisper escaped them. Little awkward boys, poor dear things, would stand in the broiling sun, outside the doors, with their eyes affectionately bent upon me in silence. I could have pressed them to my heart. It was grievous to tear myself from them. I was pained to the heart! It was unavoidable. But if I ever go, as I expect and hope, the same way again, if I do not feast my eye and my heart awhile with these ever dear people. At Macon I found a few rude people, but not one in Columbus that did not behave well. Meantime those who called were, first, Mirabeau Lamar, Esq. a cousin to the member of Congress of that name. He is a Jackson man in politics, the editor of a paper, and a very smart, intelligent man. Mr. L. is in the bloom of manhood, with a finely formed figure, fair, manly face, soft black eye, and a countenance indicative of genius and deepness of thought. His manner is prompt and graceful, and his language discovers a strength of mind, information and independence, which ranks him amongst the first men in the South.[68]

Dr. E.C. Degraffenreed (sic) is also young looking, stoutly made, with a handsome face, and an uncommon fine full dark eye. The Dr. is frank and friendly, and a perfect gentleman.[69]

Mr. Richardson is a very decent man, friendly and polite. Dr. Scott is of middle size, with a heavy brow and very delicate features—he is quite genteel. Arthur B. Davis is a light figure, thin visage, and a most amiable man.

Mr. J.C. Hall, a Yankee, is a very kind, friendly man. He was from the land of snags, and from the same my friend James Van Ness, Esq. Mr. V. is very young and a very tall man, of delicate make, with a fair face, much like his father, and a mild blue eye; he is highly polished in his manners, but there was little difference in them all. Messrs. N.F. Collins, (the latter a very modest unassuming man.) A.F. Moor, David J. Brite, and Jacob J. Moses, and many others called—a much larger turn out than at Macon, and many called after I left the place! Dear people! I trust we will meet again! They were not inferior to any of the southern gentlemen—all generous and affable, and whose kindness and respect is engraven on my heart.

But for my landlord, Mr. Dillard, I have no language that would convey an adequate idea of the man! One of the most princely of his calling—may he meet the patronage he merits.[70]

The Chattahoochie is navigable from this place to Apalachicola, 300 miles for steam-boats, nine months in the year, and for small boats all the year.

7

JAMES STUART, 1830

"No inland town of the south has increased with more rapidity than Columbus"

Aspiring travel writer James Stuart, on a prolonged tour of the United States, made his way to Columbus after traveling overland through central Georgia along a road he described as "a mere track in the forest." Having already experienced exceptionally crude accommodations, even for the day, he may have been prone to more lavish praise than warranted upon his arrival on the banks of the Chattahoochee when he was exposed to Columbus's relatively posh amenities. While it is difficult to discern any trace of hyperbole in Stuart's account of a two-year-old Columbus, it is nonetheless clear that the fledgling city stood out to him as a bastion of sophistication and modernity surrounded by a raw frontier.[71]

Stuart expressed some surprise at just how rapidly the city had become an urban center. Its many stores, churches, and public buildings of both wood and brick drew his attention, as did its scenic riverside location. It is telling that in the middle of Stuart's narrative about his visit to Columbus, however, he enters into a discussion of his observations about the unseemly institution of slavery and its role in Southern society. Columbus was founded at the head of navigation of a river system virtually tailor-made for the antebellum, slave-based cotton trade, and to a considerable extent the region in which Columbus lay tied its early development to slavery. Stuart's comments on slave law are included here as they illustrate the underpinnings of the society in which Columbus would develop.

The Stagecoach Inn in the community of Marshallville, which sat along an antebellum road east of Columbus and was photographed in the 1930s, is typical of the roadside accommodations travelers in western Georgia might have encountered in the first half of the nineteenth century. *Courtesy of the Library of Congress.*

Despite his acuity at observation, Stuart made for somewhat of an unlikely travel writer. A longtime government office worker, he unceremoniously resigned from his post and later occupied his time by ignominiously becoming embroiled in several heated exchanges over political debates in the papers. Following one particularly vitriolic episode, he engaged in a duel and killed his opponent with a pistol. Acquitted, Stuart decided to leave his native Scotland to travel abroad before starting a career in journalism. It was during this interlude that he visited Columbus, having traveled along the eastern seaboard and through middle Georgia before his arrival. The account of his experiences, simply entitled *Three Years in North America,* proved surprisingly popular and underwent multiple printings.[72]

We pick up Stuart's account after a trying and uncomfortable night in miserable quarters east of Columbus:

> We, a party consisting of six, were, first of all, shown into a separate building of one apartment, in which there was a large bed, and a blazing fire of wood, standing with their backs to which were the landlord, and a traveler who had previously arrived . . . We were both cold and hungry, but could neither procure food

nor get to a fire . . . accommodation for strangers consisted of the eating-room, and a general bed-room adjoining, and a separate bed-room, into which we had been first of all shown. Nothing more could be done than to secure a separate bed in the general sleeping room, which I accordingly did; but it was with great difficulty that I could get a couple of chairs on which to place my clothes;—a wooden bicker full of water instead of a bason; and a thing smaller than in former days a British lady's pin-cushion for the ornament of her toilet table, for a pillow! The bed itself was as wretched as possible; but, covering the bed-clothes with a great coat and sleeping in a night gown, I contrived to have as much repose as usual. There was no bolt nor lock on the door, and the boards were open to the blast. We found that General Van Rensallaer, the patron of Albany, with other passengers, had arrived by the stage from the south soon after our supper was over. How they were accommodated I cannot conceive.

Next morning we quitted this uncomfortable place, and proceeded at an early hour to Columbus, where we got a good breakfast in a comfortable hotel. A great part of the road for some days past has been a mere track in the forest, in which many of the stumps of the trees still remain. The distance from Augusta to Columbus is 247 miles; and we were in the mail-stage three days and part of the fourth. Marks are seen everywhere of the improvement of the country being quite in an incipient state. Much of the soil is good and productive; but there is also a considerable quantity of sandy gravelly land. Cotton is the great staple of the country. The sugar cane has only hitherto been cultivated for home consumption. Very little rice is grown in the State of Georgia.

The laws on the subject of slavery in the State of Georgia are as tyrannical as in any of the states. In case any slave, or free person of colour, teach any other slave, or free person of colour, to read or to write either written or printed characters, the free person of colour, or slave, is punished by fine and whipping; and a white person so offending is punished with a fine, not exceeding 500 dollars, and imprisonment in the common gaol [jail]. Any slave, or free person of colour, or any other person, circulating papers, or bringing into this state, or aiding in any manner in bringing into the state papers for the purposes of exciting to insurrection, conspiracy, or resistance among the slaves, or free persons of colour, against their owners, or the citizens, is to be punished with death . . .

Cutting off the ears and the pillory are punishments for slaves sanctioned by the legislature of Georgia; but the universal punishment is whipping. The infliction of this punishment, to the extent of twenty lashes, on the bare back, is deemed in a great variety of cases of insufficient moment to claim the intervention even of a single magistrate. Any white person, a drunken patrole, an absconding felon, or a vagabond mendicant, are supposed to possess discretion enough to interpret the laws, and to wield the cow-skin or cart-whip for their infraction; and should death ensue by accident, while this slave is thus receiving moderate correction, the constitution of Georgia kindly denominates the offence justifiable homicide.

The village of Columbus is situated on the east bank of the Chattahoochee River, immediately below the falls, which stop farther navigation. But the steamboats ply to Columbus, although 430 miles from Apalachicola Bay, in the Gulf of Mexico. Columbus is an extraordinary instance of the surprising celerity with which a town, in a favourable situation, at once becomes a considerable place in this country. It was only laid off by commissioners appointed for the purpose in the month of July 1828; and now, in March 1830, there is a population of 1500 people, three churches, a post-office, several brick buildings, and above 130 frame buildings of wood, most of them painted without, and the whole erected on a regular plan. No inland town of the south has increased with more rapidity than Columbus in substantial improvement; and none has, as I am told, a better prospect of attaining commercial importance. The Steubenville was the first steam-boat that ascended the Chattahoochee as far as Columbus, and in February 1828; but that vessel and three others have since that time been regularly plying. We arrived at Columbus on a Sunday morning; and I learned from the driver, that the mail-stage generally remained here all day on Sunday; but Mr. Crowall [*sic*], who with his brother were, I found, agents for the

United States government at Fort Mitchell, in the territory of the Creek Indians, at the distance of eleven miles from Columbus, was so very anxious to get home immediately, that I yielded to his entreaty, and agreed, after taking a walk to see the environs of Columbus and the river, to proceed to Fort Mitchell. . . .

Columbus is situated on a level piece of ground, about sixty feet above the river, which is about 250 yards wide, and the banks of which, close to the town, are extremely beautiful. The morning was clear and bright when we were there; and it seemed to me as if the whole population of the place were on the banks of the river, which were crowded with people, many of them fishing on the river edge, and others in boats on the stream. We crossed the river on a float; and on landing on the west side, found ourselves in the territory of the Creek Indians, in the State of Alabama. The Creeks here are numerous, consisting of about 20,000 persons. Their land is about 100 miles long, by sixty in breadth. Considerable part of it is of very fine quality, lying along the noble river Chattahoochee.[73]

Depiction of performance of *Pizarro* in Columbus by Solomon Smith's troupe. From *Theatrical Management in the West and South for Thirty Years Interspersed with Anecdotical Sketches* by Solomon Franklin Smith.

8

SOLOMON FRANKLIN SMITH, 1832

"The streets of Columbus were filled with gayly-dressed citizens and Creek Indians"

Solomon Franklin "Sol" Smith is one of the more celebrated writers of so-called "Old Southwest humor," a genre of character and folk-life sketches defined more by era (1830–40s) and geographic focus (Alabama, Georgia, Mississippi, Tennessee) than any conscious literary bent. The style features rare usages of dialectic, self-deprecating humor, and a healthy dose of locally flavored legend in narrative construction. The result is often an insightful account of a place in time that portrays daily life with satire but simultaneous and unusual candor. Sol Smith's account of a visit to Alabama and Georgia in 1832 is in many ways a hallmark example of the tradition; equal parts straightforward documentary and embellished tale of adventure.[74]

Smith managed a successful theatrical company and came to Columbus while on one of his barnstorming tours throughout the South. In those days the arrival of itinerant actors such as his troupe was often big news in the region's many small frontier communities, most of which could not support permanent theaters. Simply to have theatrical performances, temporary or otherwise, in a town, in many ways served as one gauge of its status. For 1832 Columbus, the performances of Smith's group would have been a highlight event in a young city just coming into its own culturally, and a measure of its growing affluence.[75]

Smith details his efforts to arrange for a performance in the city, the associated efforts undertaken in the endeavor, and the comic ending to his attempt to employ local Creek Indians in a play. In the process, we gain a bit of perspective on both social and cultural life in the early years of Columbus, and a glimpse at the types of people someone walking its streets might have encountered:

> "Georgia! Generous, hospitable Georgia! How well do I remember my sensations when first entering upon your soil! It was Sunday, and the streets of Columbus were filled with gayly-dressed citizens and Creek Indians. The arrival of a theatrical company created a decided sensation.
>
> "When do you open?" was the general question.
>
> "Next Thursday," was the response.
>
> "*Where* do you open?" was the next and most natural inquiry.
>
> "In the NEW THEATRE," was the brief but somewhat puzzling reply.
>
> Having taken possession of apartments in the Columbus Hotel, then kept by Messrs. Pomeroy and Montague, I asked that a message should be sent to the most expeditious contractor in the city. A Mr. Bates soon appeared, and in twenty minutes he had my directions. On the next Saturday the following *true* paragraph appeared in one of the newspapers:
>
> "EXPEDITION.—A theatre, 70 feet long by 40 wide, was commenced on Monday morning last by our enterprising fellow-citizen, Mr. Bates, and finished on Thursday afternoon, in season for the reception of Mr. Sol. Smith's company on that evening. A great portion of the timber, on Monday morning, waved to the breeze in its native forest; fourscore hours afterward, its massive piles were shaken by the thunder of applause in the crowded assemblage of men."
>
> Here began my acquaintance-may I not say friendship?—with Mirabeau B. Lamar, Esq., afterward President of Texas. He was a candidate for Congress—not nominated on the ticket of either party, but "on his own hook"—merely for the "excitement" it afforded him. With the same object he traveled through Texas, fought at the battle of San Jacinto, eventually submitted his name to the people of that redeemed country as a candidate for the highest office in their gift, and was elected.

Unusual Ceremonies in the Temple of the Sun

Pizarro was one of our most popular stock plays. My brother Lem's *Rolla* was his best tragic character; when dressed for the part he *looked* every inch an Indian chief. At Columbus we produced this tragedy *with real Indians for the Peruvian army.* The effect was very *striking,* but there were some unrehearsed effects not set down in the bills. I had bargained with a chief for twenty-four Creek Indians (to furnish their own bows, arrows, and tomahawks), at fifty cents each and a glass of whisky. Unfortunately for the entire success of the performance, the whisky was paid and drank in advance, causing a great degree of exhilaration among our new *supes.* They were ranged at the back of the theatre building, in an open lot, during the performance of the first act, and on the commencement of the second they were marshaled into the back door, and posted upon the stage behind the scenes. The entrance of *Rolla* was the signal for a "shout" by the company, carpenters, and scene-shifters; the Indians, supposing *their time had come,* raised such a yell as I am sure had never before been heard inside of a theatre. This outburst being quelled, the scene between *Alonzo, Cora,* and the Peruvian chief was permitted to proceed to its termination uninterrupted; but when the scene changed to the Temple of the Sun, disclosing the troops of *Rolla* (his "brave associated, partners of his toil, his feelings, and his fame") drawn up on each side of the stage in battle array, the plaudits of the audience were answered by whoops and yells that might be, and no doubt were, heard a mile off. Order being partially restored, *Rolla* addressed his army, and was greeted with another series of shouts and yells even louder than those which had preceded. Now came *my* turn to take part in the unique performance. As *High Priest of the Sun,* and followed by half a dozen virgins and as many priests, with measured step, timed to slow music, I emerged from behind the scenes, and "with solemn march" perambulated the stage, in dumb show called down a blessing on the swords of *King Ataliba* and *General Rolla,* and in the usual impressive style, looking up into the front gallery, commenced the Invocation to the Sun. Before the time for the joining in of the chorus, I found I was not entirely alone in my singing. A humming sound, at first low and mournful, and rising gradually to *forte*, greeted my ear; and when our chorus *did* join in the strain, it was quite overpowered by the rising storm of *fortissimo* sounds which were issuing from the stentorian lungs of the savages; in short, *the Indians were preparing for battle* by executing, in their most approved style, the Creek war-song and dance! To attempt stopping them we found would be a vain task; so, that, after a moment or two of hesitation, the virgins made a precipitate retreat to their dressing-rooms, where they carefully locked themselves in. The *King, Rolla*, and *Orano* stood their ground, and were compelled to submit to the new order of things. The Indians kept up their song and war-dance for full half an hour, performing the most extraordinary feats ever exhibited on a stage, in their excitement scalping *King Ataliba* (taking off his wig), demolishing the altar, and burning up the sun! As for Lem and I (*Rolla* and the *High Priest*), we joined in with them, and danced until the perspiration fairly rolled from our bodies in large streams, the savages all the time flourishing their tomahawks and knives around our heads, and performing other little playful antics not by any means agreeable or desirable. At last, to put an end to a scene which was becoming more and more tiresome as it proceeded, an order was given to drop the curtain. This stroke of policy did not stop the ceremonies, which proceeded without intermission until the savages had finished their song and dance, when, each receiving his promised half dollar, they consented to leave the house, and our play proceeded without them. Next night the same troupe came to the theatre and wanted to *assist* in the performance of MACBETH, but I most positively declined their "valuable aid." [76]

9

CARL DAVID ARFWEDSON, 1833

"Its rapid increase . . . may probably soon bring it on the grand stage of the world . . ."

Businessman and erstwhile travel writer Carl David Arfwedson set sail from Britain in 1832 on what would become a nearly two-year journey through the United States and Canada. Arfwedson's chronicle of his travels in the Chattahoochee Valley is particularly enlightening because it includes relatively indepth accounts of both the city of Columbus and the fledgling community across the river from which Phenix City, Alabama, traces its origins. The two towns share a symbiotic historical relationship that has often been overlooked and has been, at various times, both controversial and complementary. Like many visitors, Arfwedson found the evidence of maturity in early Columbus somewhat astonishing and appears convinced its future held great promise.[77]

He was less sanguine, however, when evaluating the people of the young town. He held the frontier community's society to be generally of a lower caliber than that of more established American settlements, and blamed the situation in no small part on its location at the very fringe of "civilization" in Georgia. Across the river to the west lay the Creek Nation, and it is with some truth that Arfwedson surmised that the area attracted troublemakers and outlaws—Creeks aside. Arfwedson seemed both troubled and surprised by the trafficking in human slaves he witnessed just outside of town—his is one of the earliest accounts of the slave trade in Columbus.

We pick up Arfwedson's journey the morning after the wagon in which he was traveling broke down just outside Columbus,

A slave coffle. *Courtesy of the Library of Congress.*

an all too frequent occurrence on the rough roads leading into the town:

> . . .Without waiting for the break of day, I continued my journey on foot, in company with one of the passengers well acquainted with the road. During this compulsory promenade, I had frequent opportunities of contemplating the wild and uniform appearance of these uncultivated regions. From a soil almost exclusively of sand, rose a close dark wood, the height of whose trees bespoke venerable age . . . Nearer to Columbus, the country became more hilly; the Alleghany Mountain chain, which may be called the back-bone of North America, here commences in a long series of sloping hills, above and round which the road winds in various directions.
>
> It was at the foot of one of these hills that I fell in with a gang (as they are called) of slaves, on their march to New Orleans, for sale. The slave-trader had chained them two and two together, and so disposed of them during the few hours in the night allowed for rest after the day's fatigue, that none of them could possibly escape the watchful eyes of the owner or his assistant.

A great number of these miserable beings were seated round a large fire, attentively listening to each other's narratives: others were lying in groups, absorbed in profound sleep. At the further extremity, near a tree, was the slave-trader himself, looking sternly at his victims, and now and then roaring to them to be quiet. He was not, however, able to quell the general mirth that prevailed, occasioned by the lively anecdotes related by a young slave, about twenty, to his companions in misfortune: laughter and signs of approbation continued without interruption. Yes, bursts of laughter made the whole wood ring. Who would have supposed that these were slaves, going to a market for sale? Without being perceived, we approached this singular group. They were all without any head-covering, but pretty decently dressed in linen clothes, in my opinion rather too light for winter, but with which they seemed perfectly satisfied. Real joy was expressed in every countenance, and they gave way to fits of laughter, which made their eyes sparkle with tears . . .

On the eastern bank of the River Chattahoochee is a small town called Columbus, which, founded so recently as the year 1828, has not yet attained so much celebrity as to have a place allotted to it in all the maps of the United States. Numbers of Americans know not that such a town exists . . . Columbus still ranks among the smaller towns, without any pretension to fame, though it may not be doomed to remain long in obscurity. Its rapid increase in population, wealth, and trade, may probably soon bring it on the grand stage of the world . . .

The situation of the town is on the confines of Georgia and Alabama, and on the river Chattahoochee, which is navigable as far as the Gulf of Mexico. This river, on which four steamers are continually plying, has been of such infinite advantage to this place, that it may already be called a flourishing town. The population exceeded two thousand, and among them were several that might be denominated wealthy. The number of the inhabitants was augmenting monthly, and the increase of commerce, I was assured, was in the same proportion. Carpenters, masons, and workmen of every kind, were never without employment, and could not erect houses fast enough. Streets, which in 1828 were only marked out, were now so filled with loaded wagons that it was next to impossible to pass. The principal street which traverses the city, following the course of the river is, like the rest, not paved, but has so many shops filled with a variety of goods, such a number of neat houses, and, finally, in the mornings such a concourse of people, Christians and Indians, that it can hardly be believed that it is the same street which was only marked out in 1828. Most of the houses were of wood, and some of brick: a few in the English style, others again in the Grecian style. The hotels are, perhaps, the worst buildings in the town: I resided in one, the staircase of which bore a strong resemblance to a fire-ladder, and the bed-room, although provided with window-frames, had no panes of glass in them.

Commerce is also on the increase, and will be still more flourishing, when the neighbouring tract of land in Alabama, bought by the State from the Indians, but which they had not yet quitted, is brought into cultivation. At the northern extremity of the town, the river forms several falls, which are made available for working cotton-factories. The goods are conveyed by the steamers to a seaport at the mouth of the river called Apalachicola, where they are re-shipped for exportation.

The manners of the people were uncouth to a degree, which made it equally disagreeable and hazardous for a civilized person to remain in Columbus. Many individuals, there called gentlemen, would in other places receive a very different appellation. The proximity of the Indian territory on the other side of the river contributed not a little to the toleration among the inhabitants of a certain number of loose persons, on which account morals were at the lowest ebb. Opposite to the town, on the Alabama shore, a number of dissolute people had founded a village, for which their lawless pursuits and atrocious misdeeds had procured the name Sodom. Scarcely a day passed without some human blood being shed in its vicinity; and not satisfied with murdering each other, they cross the river clandestinely, and pursue their bloody vocation even in Columbus. Peaceable citizens are thus often attacked, not only in the streets or in the woods, but in their own houses: in vain do they look for reparation or protection from the authorities of the town. The delinquents of Sodom are exempt from all prosecution, their village being situated on the Indian territory, and as such under no control. Temerity, courage, and boldness, alone command respect from these banditti: mildness, virtue, and beauty, are in their eyes so many contemptible attributes, which they conceive they have a right to violate with impunity. The manner of living has meanwhile, by the frequent occurrence of these atrocities, acquired a degree of insecurity, which obliges every one to carry arms about his person, and to be prepared for defence at a moment's warning.[78]

When laws have so little power to protect the lives of citizens, necessity makes it obligatory to obtain justice by personal efforts; and, when this alternative unfortunately occurs, passions generally gain the ascendency, and, as a consequence, the contest on both sides too often terminates in blood. The most trifling difference not unfrequently occasions murders of the blackest dye, and when the crime is consummated, the offender hastens across the river to Sodom, boasting of his deed, and scoffing at the lamentations of the relations and friends of the murdered victim . . . With such neighbors, it certainly is not surprising that the citizens of Columbus should preserve a certain uncouthness of manners, peculiar to a place that has just sprung up in a forest, but which, from its rapid progress, ought to have already disappeared, if the vicinity of Sodom had not a certain degree retarded the advance of civilization . . . After remaining in this town a few days, I continued my journey towards the West in a carriage drawn by one horse, accompanied by a boy seven years old as guide.[79]

Tyrone Power in character. *Courtesy of the Library of Congress.*

10

TYRONE POWER, 1834

"Nowhere in this South country have I yet seen a place which promises more of the prosperity increasing wealth can bestow"

Tyrone Power's description of his visit to western Georgia characterizes Columbus as a city in a state of transition from isolated frontier community to becoming a pivotal waypoint in a well-developed trade and transportation nexus. Power had certainly seen enough of the world to make such an observation, for the Irish-born actor was among the most famous people of his day and had visited cities and stages across Europe and America. Indeed, Power's ability to interpret the things he witnessed and his facility to relate them to an audience were expressed through a number of popular plays he wrote himself.[80]

It is in Power's account of his extensive travels in the United States, *Impressions of America,* in which his observations of an 1834 visit to Columbus appear. Although a summary of the people and places he encountered on his trips to cities and stages across America, the book also reveals Power's fascination with America's dynamic society and the rapid changes sweeping through the nation at the time. In few places did he witness such a rapid evolution from wilderness to urban living as was happening on the banks of the Chattahoochee.

The chronicle of his sojourn juxtaposes the newfound wealth of the city—rendered almost ostentatious by its incongruity with its wilderness setting—with the relatively primitive condition of the community of "Sodom" (forerunner of Phenix City) on the opposite bank of the river and the distressed condition of the Creek people who resided there alongside the rowdy American settlers. The portrait Power paints is unvarnished and not entirely flattering: Columbus as an unpolished town on the make, Sodom as a haven for outlaws who seemingly lived beyond the reach of legal authorities, and the downtrodden Creeks reduced by poverty and getting by on the beneficence of the new arrivals to their ancestral lands. Power's observations are only a few half-focused snapshots of a complicated mosaic, yet they capture a moment in time and vividly present the place and its people as few others do:

> At the hour of two, A.M. we reached the city of Columbus, on the Chattahoochee, the river dividing Alabama from Georgia. Here we halted for a day and a night; and this time I employed, in company with my two New York fellow-travellers, in paying a visit to the Choctaw [sic] tribe of Indians, who possess a reserve lying west of the river.[81]
>
> We procured three stout nags, and early in the morning crossed the very fine bridge which spans this stream close to the falls. On the Alabama side we found ourselves within a wild-looking village, scattered through the edge of the forest, bearing the unattractive name of Sodom; few of its denizens were yet stirring; they are composed chiefly of "minions o' the moon," outlaws from the neighbouring States. Gamblers, and other desperate men, here find security from their numbers, and from the vicinity of a thinly inhabited Indian country, whose people hold them in terror, yet dare not refuse them a hiding-place. These bold outlaws, I was informed, occasionally assemble to enjoy an evening's frolic in Columbus, on which occasion they cross the dividing bridge in force, all armed to the teeth: the warrants in the hands of the U.S. Marshal are at such times necessarily suspended, since to execute a caption would require a muster greater than any within his command. If unmolested, the party usually proceed to the nearest hotel, drink deeply, make what purchases they require for the ladies of their colony, retire peaceably into the territory, wherein their present rule is by report absolute. The condition of this near community, and the crimes perpetrated by its members, were alluded to within the town with a mingled sentiment of detestation and fear.
>
> The condition of the majority of these poor people (the Creeks) seemed wretched in the extreme: most of

the families were living in wigwams, built of bark or green boughs, of the frailest and least comfortable construction; not an article of furniture, except a kettle, was in the possession of this class. A few, however, were here who had erected log-houses, cleared a little land, and were also in the possession of a stove or two; we halted at a group of four of these little dwellings, where, under a shed, a fine negro wench was occupied frying bacon and making cakes of wheaten flour for her master's supper, who, she informed us, was absent on a hunting expedition. Within the log-huts sat the squaws of the party, all busily employed sewing beads on moccasins, or ornamenting deer-skin pouches, after the fashion of the dames of old in the absence of their true knights; our guide addressed these ladies roughly enough; but without eliciting any reply more encouraging than a sort of "Ugh! Ugh!" unaccompanied by a single look. The negro girl, however, had not adopted the taciturnity of the tribe, but readily chatted with us, explaining, amongst other matters, the nature of the contents of the boiler, whose savoury smell greatly attracted our attention. She said it was composed of Indian corn, boiled a great deal and slowly, with only a little salt for seasoning; affirming, that the Indians preferred this simple dish to all other dainties. For myself, I gave a decided vote in favour of fried rashers, and the nice little cakes baked in the ashes: of these we partook freely, at the solicitation of the good-humoured cook, who, with right Indian hospitality, assured us there was plenty more.

Returning, we encountered several members of this tribe who had been passing the day in Columbus; some were on foot, others riding, but all more or less elevated; a few of the women were good-looking, and to their credit, all of them sober. As we repassed Sodom, the sound of revelry proclaimed the orgies resumed. The rain, which had hitherto held up, once more began to descend with a determination of purpose that boded us no good: we spurred over the covered bridge and were soon after housed again in Georgia . . .

During the afternoon I walked about this thriving frontier town, despite a smart shower: the stores were well supplied, the warehouses filled with cotton, and in all quarters were groups of the neighboring planters busied in looking after the sale of their produce, and making such purchases as their families required. Numerous parties of Indians, —Creeks and Choctaws, —roamed about from place to place, mostly drunk, or seeking to become so as quickly as possible: with each party of the natives I observed a negro-man, the slave of some one present, but commonly well dressed in the European manner, having an air of superior intelligence to his masters, and evidently exercising over them the power and influence derived from superior knowledge: the negroes, in fact, appeared the masters, and the red-men the slaves.

Along the river-front of the town, a situation wildly beautiful, I observed several dwellings of mansion-like proportions, and others of a similar character in progress. I should say, that nowhere in this South country have I yet seen a place which promises more of the prosperity increasing wealth can bestow than this; or one that, from all I learned, is more wanting in all that men usually consider most worth possessing,—personal security, reasonable comfort, and well-executed law. In place of these, affrays ending in blood are said to be frequent, apprehensions few, acquittal next to certain even in the event of trial, and the execution of a white man a thing unknown.

In the midst of all this, be it understood, I do not consider that a traveler runs the least risk; robbery, or murder for the sake of mere plunder, never occurs; and to a stranger the rudest of these frontier spirits are usually exceedingly civil; but idleness, hot blood, and frequent stimulants make gambling or politics ready subjects for quarrels, and, as the parties always go armed, an affray is commonly fatal to some of those concerned.

As the population steadily advances, these wild spirits melt away before it, some becoming good citizens, others clearing out before the onward march of civilization; their sway is therefore yearly decreasing in force within the States, their sphere becoming limited in proportion as persons interested in the support of law increase; already, each season, numbers seek freedom from restraint within the Mexican territory, where an infusion of such blood will be productive of strange events in Texas . . .[82]

11

JOHN H. B. LATROBE, 1834

"The sound of music and the tread of merry feet came across the square of the town"

One of most interesting and talented individuals to record his visit to antebellum Columbus was John Hazlehurst Boneval Latrobe. Son of noted architect Benjamin Henry Latrobe, the younger Latrobe became something of a Renaissance man. An accomplished attorney by trade, he also dabbled in art, architecture, and writing—all to some level of acclaim. He designed the base of the memorial sculpture to Thaddeus Kosciuszko which stands at West Point; planned portions of the Basilica of the National Shrine of the Assumption of the Blessed Virgin Mary in Baltimore; published a legal reference book, and rubbed shoulders with visionaries of his age such as Samuel F. B. Morse and Edgar Allan Poe. Interested in seemingly everything that came within his survey, he also helped organize the Maryland Historical Society and became active in the African Colonization Society. He is credited with coining the name for the African republic of Liberia, which served as a destination for former slaves that the group transported, after noting the Latin term for "free man" was "liber."[83]

While Latrobe traveled extensively throughout his life, he began keeping journals of his trips only after his wife died in 1831. On many of his journeys from that point forward, he began keeping notes and even occasionally making sketches of things he encountered. He remarried in December 1832 to Virginia Charlotte Claiborne of Natchez, Mississippi, the daughter of Old Southwest luminary Ferdinand Leigh Claiborne and niece of political figure W. C. C. Claiborne. He found his jour-

John H. B. Latrobe. *Courtesy of the Library of Congress.*

neys to his wife's Deep South home fascinating. His journal of a trip to New Orleans in 1834, where he was planning to spend the winter owing to his wife's poor health at the time, contains the account of a visit to Columbus:[84]

> At Fort Mitchell we got an addition of two passengers which filled our coach. The one was a talking boasting fellow who wanted to enter into an argument with me on the subject of the Bank of the United States, & other disputable matters. He annoyed me woefully, for I was sleepy and he had nothing to say worth keeping awake to hear, and after getting from him all the useful information about the country that he possessed, I let him

talk on and went to my dreams, his garrulity notwithstanding. His companion was a modest well behaved & very handsome man who had walked to Fort Mitchell from the Chattahoochee river, where he had been just able to save his life. The steamboat, Van Buren, on which he had been a passenger having caught fire in the night, when loaded with cotton and burnt to the waters edge. He seemed impressed with a deep sense of the danger he had run, and was enormously more annoyed than I was with the inconsequential babbling of the man along side of him. This last, I believe, for I was asleep, (a) great part of the time continued to prate until the sound of his voice was drowned by the rolling of the wheels across the wooden Bridge of the Chattahoochie at Columbus.[85]

At one oclock we crossed the river and reached Columbus. This is a large and thriving town in Georgia at the Falls of the Chattahoochie, which empties into the Appalachicola, and through that finds its way to the Gulf of Mexico. The Bridge across it at Columbus is built of wood, on stone piers, and is after Town's plan. Steam boats ply regularly up to the town and the rich and improving country in the neighbourhood well adapted to the culture of cotton, furnishes them with ample employment.... Appalachicola will no doubt make rapid strides and become a place of trade only second to the cities of New Orleans & Mobile—for there is a back country to support it which is daily increasing in wealth and population.

It was too late when we reached Columbus to get any thing to eat at the Tavern. To pass away the time and overcome the cravings of my appetite I determined to shave, and put on clean linen. This after some difficulty I accomplished, and felt more refreshed than I had anticipated, even. In some of my memoranda of former journeys I have I think pronounced an eulogium upon clean shirts and a smooth chin for traveler. Experience confirms what I then said. I was a happy man this evening. I even felt like going over to the Tavern opposite and praying admission to a ballroom, from which the sound of music and the tread of merry feet came across the square of the town to the cold and comfortless apartment in which I had performed my ablutions.

We got rid of our talker at Columbus, and our shipwrecked friend left us: but their places were filled by gentlemen who were bound Northwardly. At three oclock in the morning of the 11th December we left Columbus. I went to sleep forthwith notwithstanding the wind & rain which came in certain holes in the curtain next me, and did not wake until we stopped . . . This part of Georgia promises well and is by far the most interesting of any of the country I have travelled through, since leaving Mobile.

→ 12 ←

GEORGE WILLIAM FEATHERSTONHAUGH, 1835

"... the street was swarming with drunken Indians, and young prostitutes, both Indian and white, a sufficient indication of the manners of the place"

The first official US geologist, English-born George William Featherstonhaugh (pronounced "Fanshaw,") received his appointment in 1834 to produce geological surveys of several Southern and Midwestern states in order to determine their mineral resources. Possessed of an intense curiosity about natural phenomena, Featherstonhaugh's report of his remarkable journey, *Excursion Through the Slave States,* presents evidence of his scientific acumen alongside a treasure trove of accounts of the people and lifestyles he encountered on the road.[86]

Featherstonhaugh's brief account of a day spent in the Columbus area in 1835 illuminates in straightforward fashion the perspective of visitors to the city. Through his vivid description of the sometimes rather miserable accommodations afforded travelers and the unflattering first impression of segments of the local population met along the streets, readers are introduced to a rough-and-tumble frontier town where prostitutes and drunks boldly walked the streets. His is certainly not the only account to disparage the amenities and manners encountered in "noisy taverns" and sidewalks of Columbus, and the crudeness of both speaks to daily life in the community. Despite what could easily have been a bad experience, however, it is worth noting that Featherstonhaugh still described the city as "pretty," and the Chattahoochee as a "fine" stream crossed

George William Featherstonhaugh. *Courtesy of the Minnesota Historical Society.*

by an "excellent" bridge. Clearly in the 1830s Columbus was a dynamic place that offered something for those looking for both the best and worst in this developing Southern city:

> In the afternoon we reached the Chatahoochie, it having taken us four days to travel a distance of ninety miles. This fine stream is crossed by an excellent bridge, and divides the State of Georgia from the Creek territory now forming part of Alabama. On the opposite bank is the pretty town of Columbus, in Georgia, where we stopped for the night at a noisy tavern, which seemed to be a general boarding-house for the town.

My first care was to secure places for the mail-stage in the morning; the next, to hasten to the Falls of the Chatahoochie, about a mile from Columbus, where I had the pleasure of meeting the gneiss rocks again in place, and of seeing this fine river tumble over them just as it does at Fredericburgh and Richmond, in Virginia: indeed, there is a strong scenic resemblance betwixt the falls of all the rivers on the east side of the chain which fronts the Atlantic.

After gratifying my curiosity, I recrossed the bridge to the Indian side of the Chatahoochie, where I saw a great many huts, and some dwellings apparently belonging to white persons. Here I found the lowest stage of drunkenness and debauchery, prevailing to such an extent that the settlement had acquired the nickname of Sodom; and on my return into Columbus the street was swarming with drunken Indians, and young prostitutes, both Indian and white, a sufficient indication of the manners of the place.

Having reached the tavern again, we endeavoured to get something to eat, and were told to wait until the supper-bell rang; which having done with great patience, we moved, as soon as the tumultuous rush common upon such occasions was effected, to the supper-table; but it was so full that it was quite impossible to get a seat there, neither was there another chair or bench in the room; so, knowing it would serve no purpose to show any impatience, we remained standing and looking on. The art of bolting was practiced here with as much success as I had seen it done at any other place, and in less than ten minutes every man without exception had gone back again to the bar-room; a circumstance that would have given us unalloyed pleasure, if they had not taken every scrap that had been set on the table along with them. We now made our wants known; and the mistress of the house, learning that we were the two "men" that had come from the "nation" in a carriage, very obligingly ordered some food to be produced for us, which, after a little more patience, we had the satisfaction of eating alone.

We left Columbus, January 17, at 5½ A.M., keeping on the edge of the gneiss, which is covered with sand, gravel, and clay, bearing oak, hickory (Juglans), and pine-trees. During the day we got upon the red lands, formed apparently by the decomposition of primary ferruginous slates, and proceeded on over what is called a rolling and broken country. At the end of fifteen miles we stopped at Ellerslie to breakfast, and were heartily glad we should not have to encounter any more of the distressing scenes we had left behind, for we had now got into a white community, if a population can properly be called so where nine out of ten are black.

➔ 13 ⟵

HARRIET MARTINEAU, 1835

"It bears the appearance of being a thriving, spacious, handsome village, well worth stopping to see"

Harriet Martineau, aware of Basil Hall's famous visit to Columbus as it was being laid out, professed a desire to see "how the place had got on" since his sojourn when she begins the chronicle of her time on the banks of the Chattahoochee. Judging by her account, it had "gotten on" pretty well. Martineau found it a thriving young city in a beautiful setting, even if plagued by violence, mediocre hotels, and abysmal roads. The beauty of the Chattahoochee captivated Martineau, and the exotic presence of Creek Indians milling around town transfixed her. The novel sight of Creeks in the environs of Columbus rarely escaped comment by European travelers.[87]

Martineau was uniquely situated to provide an account of life in Columbus. Widely credited as the first female sociologist, her writings—including documentaries of her travels and examinations of the influence of major world religions, as well as forays into fiction—evidence a broad education and a deep-seated interest in pursuing a holistic understanding of society. Her account of Columbus appeared in perhaps her best-known volume, *Society in America*. The book achieved some level of renown—or infamy, depending on one's point of view—for its harsh criticism of both the institution of slavery and the place of women in society. Within this context of international societal critique is found the following well-rounded sketch of the sights and sounds of a city in its first decade of existence:[88]

Engraving of Harriet Martineau, after a painting by A. Chappel published in *The Masterpiece Library of Short Stories*, 1873. Unknown artist. Engraving (c. 1873); portrait (c. 1850).

When we drew near to Columbus, Georgia, we were struck with amazement at the stories that were told, and the anecdotes that were dropped, in the stage, about recent attempts on human life in the neighbourhood; and at the number of incidents of the same kind which were the news of the day along the road. Our driver from Macon had been shot at, in attempting to carry off a young lady. A gentleman, boarding in the hotel at Columbus, was shot in the back, in the street, and laid by for months. No inquiry was made, or nothing came of it. The then present governor of the State of Mississippi had recently stood over to combatants, pistol in hand, to see fair play. This *was* stated as a remarkable fact. The landlord of the house where we stopped to breakfast on the day we were to reach Columbus, April 9th, 1835, was, besides keeping a house of entertainment, a captain of militia, and a member of the legislature of Georgia. He was talking over with his guests a late case of homicide in a feud between the Myers and Macklimore families. He declared that he would have laws like those of the Medes and Persians against homicide; and, in the same breath, said that if he were a Myers, he would shoot Mr. Macklimore and all his sons.

We arrived at Columbus before sunset, and determined to stay a day to see how the place had got on since Captain Hall saw it cut out of the woods, ten years before. During the evening, I could do nothing but watch the Indians from my window. The place swarmed with them; a few Choctaws, and the rest Creeks. A sad havoc has taken place among them since; and this neighbourhood has been made the scene of a short but fierce war. But all looked fair and friendly when we were there. Groups of Indians were crouching behind another, with their hair, growing low on the forehead, loose, or tied at the back of the head, forming a fine contrast with the young lady who had presided at our breakfast-table at five that morning, with her long hair braided and adorned with brilliant combs, while her fingers shone in pearl and gold rings. These squaws carried large Indian baskets on their backs, and shuffled along, barefooted, while their lords paced before them, well mounted; or, if walking, gay with blue and red clothing and embroidered leggings, with tufts of hair at the knees, while pouches and white fringes dangled about them. They looked like grave merry-andrews; or, more still, like solemn fanatical harvest men going out for largess. By eight o'clock they had all disappeared; but the streets were full of them again the next morning.

Our hostess was civil, and made no difficulty about giving us a late breakfast by ourselves, in consideration of our fatigues. Before one o'clock we dined, in company with seventy-five persons, at one long table. The provisions were good, but ill-cooked; and the knives so blunt, that it was a mystery to me how the rest of the company obtained so quick a succession of mouthfuls as they did.

The Chattahoochee, on whose banks Columbus stands, is unlike any river I saw in the United States, unless it be some parts of the Susquehanna. Its rapids, overhung by beech and pine woods, keep up a perpetual melody, grateful alike to the ear of the white and the red man. It is broad and full, whirling over and around the rocks with which it is studded, and under the frail wooden foot-bridge which spans a portion of its width, between the shore and a pile of rocks in the middle of the channel. On this foot-bridge I stood, and saw a fish caught in a net laid among the eddies. A dark fisherman stood on each little promontory; and a group was assembled about some canoes in a creek on the opposite Alabama shore, where the steepness of the hills seemed scarcely to allow a foothold between the rushing water and the ascent. The river is spanned by a long covered bridge, which we crossed the same night on our way into Alabama.

There are three principal streets in Columbus, with many smaller, branching out into the forest. Some pretty bits of greensward are left, here and there, with a church, or a detached house upon each—village-like. There are some good houses, five hotels, and a population of above 2,000—as nearly as I could make out among the different accounts of the accession of inhabitants since the census. The stores looked creditably stocked; and a great many gentlemanly men were to be seen in the streets. It bears the appearance of being a thriving, spacious, handsome village, well worth stopping to see.

We left it, at seven in the evening, by the long bridge, at the other end of which we stopped for the driver to hold a parley, about a parcel, with a woman, who spoke almost altogether in oaths. A gentleman in the stage remarked, that we must have got quite to the end of the world. The roads were as bad as roads could be; and we rolled from side to side so incessantly, as to obviate all chance of sleeping. The passengers were very patient during the hours of darkness; but, after daylight, they seemed to think they had been long enough employed in shifting their weight to keep the coach on its four wheels. "I say, driver," cried one, "you won't upset us, now daylight is come?" "Driver," shouted another, "keep this side up." "Gentlemen," replied the driver, "I shall mind nothing you say till the ladies begin to complain." A reply equally politic and gallant.[89]

14

JAMES SILK BUCKINGHAM, 1839

"... there are some excellent, honourable families living there ...; but the great bulk of the community furnish some of the worst specimens of character"

From January to June of 1839, celebrated English author, journalist, lecturer, politician, activist, and world traveler James Silk Buckingham toured the Southern states in preparation for a grand narrative of a journey "through that portion of the North American republic, in which the institution of slavery still exists, and to which, its supporters and defenders still cling, with a tenacity as much to be deplored as it is to be wondered at." Acclaimed for his travel writings providing astute cultural and political observations in such diverse places as India, Canada, and the Middle East, Buckingham enjoyed a world-wide audience and had already penned two volumes focusing on American society in the Northern states by the time of his visit to the South.[90]

Buckingham had become an outspoken opponent of slavery as an institution he deemed ill-suited to the enlightened age in which he lived. In seeking specifically to explore the state of slavery in the American South, he hoped to expose, in a manner displaying "fairness and equity," the "wretched condition of the great body of the African race throughout the South; and of the reckless indifference to human life." When finally published in 1842, however, the book, *The Slave States of America*, evidenced as much sarcasm and condescension as it did fairness or equity. Yet, it revealed Buckingham to be a careful observer with an uncanny knack of taking the true temperature of the regions he visited, and

James Silk Buckingham. *Courtesy of the National Portrait Gallery, London. Attributed to Clara S. Lane, Primary Collection, NPG 236.*

it showed him to be a meticulous researcher who provided remarkably accurate details of events about which he wrote.[91]

It is both ironic and revealing that Buckingham's comments on his brief stay in Columbus focused less on the institution of slavery than on the sordid history of Indian removal in the surrounding region. The saga of the signing of the treaty by which the Creeks relinquished claim to the area and subsequently were swindled out of property promised to them in Alabama—in large part by Columbus-based speculators—is a sad but significant one in local history. Through a variety of devious machinations including fraud, bribery, and violence, the Creeks were in short order relieved of the last vestige of their ancestral homeland after the signing of the Treaty of Cusseta. With them gone or going, American planters and their slaves moved into the region en masse, helping to expand the plantation economy across the Chattahoochee Valley. Buckingham's attention to this developing situation—still being sorted out at the time of his visit—captures the spirit of the times and brings to our attention the troubled circumstances surrounding Columbus's formative years. The portrait he paints is not flattering. He found the city an exceptionally crude place that contained many rough-edged citizens complicit in one of the most shameful episodes in national history. Mixed in with commentary on Creek removal is one of the most complete descriptions of Columbus as it appeared to travelers in the 1830s, reading at times as much like a city directory as a narrative of a visit:

> It is not more than eleven years since the first house in Columbus was built, yet there is now a population of about 4,000 persons, of whom 3,000 are whites and 1,000 blacks and coloured people; the fewness of the latter, in comparison with most of the Southern towns, arises from the fact that it is not so much an agricultural place as Montgomery, Macon, or Augusta, but chiefly commercial, and its principal residents are adventurers from the New England States.[92]
>
> There are five churches in Columbus, the Episcopal, Methodist, Presbyterian, Baptist, and Roman Catholic; they are each small, and neither of them has a congregation exceeding 200. A wretched theatre, recently established, and said to be as wretchedly supplied with actors, is better attended than either of the churches; and races, balls, and the gaming table seem more popular here than religion. There is a Lyceum, but it numbers less than 100 members, and it has its gratuitous lectures delivered from time to time in the Methodist church, from inability or unwillingness to spare the funds necessary to erect a suitable building.
>
> There are two principal hotels in Columbus, the Oglethorpe and the City hotel, and several subordinate ones. We passed the few days of our stay at the former, and found it as disagreeable, as that at Montgomery had been the reverse. In this, as in most of the American hotels, the master and mistress seemed wholly indifferent to every department of the business, except making high charges and receiving the payments. One rarely or ever see them at any part of the day, as they have their private rooms, and might be taken for strangers or guests, rather than managers of the con-

cern. All is left to the slaves, who constitute the only servants here, and all is accordingly neglected . . . The common deficiency of washbasins and jugs, of towels and glasses, with broken locks, broken panes, and curtainless windows, was here more than usually apparent; and there being but few attendants—and these unskillful and unwilling—and no bell or other method of calling them, the traveler must help himself as well as he can.

It was remarkable that this hotel was spoken of, far and near, as being provided with "silver forks;" and as this was thought a great luxury and refinement, it was presumed that everything else was on a corresponding scale. But this was a most erroneous conclusion; silver forks indeed there were, but the spoons were pewter, and the tea-service of queen's-metal, while the fare at table was so bad, that though we had been now tolerably well trained into the miserable living of country hotels in the South, this was almost unbearable, and we had some difficulty, indeed, in mustering appetites to eat sufficient for mere subsistence—comfort or enjoyment was quite out of the question. Though our own tastes were of the simplest kind, yet where the bread is but half baked, the butter rancid, the milk sour, the water dirty, the eggs stale, and every kind of meat and poultry as tough as leather, it is difficult for even persons of simple tastes to live tolerably . . . We had stipulated for a private sitting-room, and one was nominally awarded to us; but they could not comprehend the propriety of preventing other persons from coming and sitting in it, if they chose . . .

There are three weekly newspapers in Columbus—the *Inquirer*, *Argus*, and *Sentinel*—but only one bookseller's and stationer's shop, and that so poorly furnished, that we could not procure even a sheet of drawing-paper, or card-board, of the smallest size—no kind of drawing materials being ever inquired for, as we were told; and their supply of books was ill-assorted and scanty. Everything connected with literature or the arts seemed indeed to be at a lower ebb in Columbus, than we had found it in any town in which we had made any stay in the United States, which is the more remarkable, when it is considered that its inhabitants are chiefly settlers from New England . . .

In the sitting-room which we occupied at Columbus, was a full-length portrait of General M'Intosh, the late chief of the Creek nation, habited in that singular mixture of European and Indian costume . . . His character appeared to be held in the highest esteem by the American residents in Columbus, chiefly because many of them had profited by his treachery . . .[93]

. . . force was employed to compel the Indians to remove. This led, as might have been expected, to resistance; and in the war thus created, the greatest atrocities were perpetrated on either side. Columbus and its neighbourhood had its full share of the horrors of this bloody campaign; the recollection of which, indeed, is so fresh in the memory of most of the inhabitants here, that they seem to feel a renewal of the terrors inspired by the original events while describing them to others. . . These events happened about three years ago only, but though the greater part of the Creek Indians have been actually removed, and their lands are now held by American purchasers, yet the Creek war can hardly yet be said to be at an end; for a number of fugitive Indians, who would not join the removing party, still continue in the territory, and pursue a sort of guerilla warfare against the whites, whenever an opportunity offers for revenge. Even now, in May, 1839, during our actual stay at Columbus, the following events occurred, and were made public in the Columbus papers.

. . . It was a common practice with the whites, who had congregated here as land speculators, at the conclusion of M'Intosh's treaty before mentioned, to . . . first decoy one of the Indians of the Creek tribe, by prevailing on him to drink whiskey; and when they had got him thus completely under their control, they would procure two other Indians, and two unprincipled whites as witnesses, get the Indians to swear in their presence to a document describing the boundaries of certain plots of land, as being his property, and assigning it over to the white purchaser, for a large consideration, in money, and in goods. They would then take him before a district-court, or magistrate, who would publicly ratify this sale; and after paying the Indian, perhaps, a twentieth of the sum set forth in the document of sale, they would get the white witnesses to swear that he had been paid the whole amount in their presence, and had afterwards squandered or lost it . . . The influence of such transactions as these fraudulent land-purchases, on the general state of society at Columbus, is felt very powerfully at present, and will continue to be felt, no doubt, for years to come.

That there are some excellent, honourable families living there, and in its neighbourhood, is undoubtedly true; but the great bulk of the community furnish some of the worst specimens of character, and the reputation of Columbus stands at a low estimate . . .[94]

After being detained longer than we wished, from the difficulty of getting conveyances for Macon, we considered ourselves fortunate in being at length released from our confinement at Columbus.[95]

→ 15 ←

SIR CHARLES LYELL, 1846

"Northern settlers are compelled to preserve a discreet silence about such grievances when in the society of Southern slave-owners, but are open and eloquent in decanting upon them to a stranger."

Failing eyesight allegedly caused young up-and-coming lawyer Charles Lyell to change his career and pursue his passion of science instead. Perhaps the copious amounts of reading of legal texts were more than his weak vision could handle. If the story is true, his writing demonstrates clearly that his limitations were purely physical, for he could still clearly see the makeup of people and the societies of which they were a part.[96]

An associate of Charles Darwin, Lyell had become internationally recognized as an authority on geology at the time he visited Columbus in the 1840s. He is most widely remembered as the author of *Principles of Geology*, which won him great acclaim for bringing the concept of uniformitarianism—the idea that the earth was shaped by processes that are still in operation—to the public conscious. His travel volumes, however, featuring unvarnished analyses of the societies that he encountered on his extended journeys in North America, reveal both his passionate fascination with the natural environment and his remarkable ability to summarize the essence of the communities he visited even during brief stays.

He wrote his first major travel volume, *Travels in North America*, following a wide-ranging trip throughout the eastern coast of North America from Nova Scotia down to the Carolinas in 1841–42. His second trip to North America in 1845–46 included several stops in the Southern states.[97]

Sir Charles Lyell. *Courtesy of the Library of Congress.*

His remarks about his trip through western Georgia naturally feature commentary on the geology of the area interspersed with relatively common observations illustrating the hazards and inconveniences of travel during the era. With piercing insight, he also offers thoughts on the effects of urban growth on the environment and the impact of the institution of slavery on the economic life of the city. Lyell's account is one of the most profound and provocative portraits of Columbus produced by visitors of which we have record, written as the area made its rapid transition from frontier community to Deep South industrial city. We pick up Lyell's account on the road to Columbus from Macon:

> For the first time, we remarked that our friends, on parting, wished us a *safe* journey, instead of a pleasant one, as usual . . . Our coach was built on a plan almost universal in America, and like those used in some parts of France, with three seats, the middle one provided with a broad leather strap, to lean back upon. The best places are given to the ladies, and a husband is seated next to his wife. There are no outside passengers, except occasionally one sitting by the driver's side. We were often called upon, on a sudden, to throw our weight first on the right, and then on the left side, to balance the vehicle and prevent an upset, when one wheel was sinking into a deep rut. Sometimes all the gentlemen were ordered to get out in the dark, and walk in the wet and muddy road. The coachman would then whip on his steeds over a fallen tree or deep pool, causing tremendous jolts, so that my wife was thrown first against the roof, and then against the side of the lightened vehicle, having almost reason to envy those who were merely splashing through the mud. To sleep was impossible, but at length, soon after daybreak, we found ourselves entering the suburbs of Columbus; and the first sight we saw there was a long line of negroes, men, women, and boys, well dressed and very merry, talking and laughing, who stopped to look at our coach. On inquiry, we were told that it was a gang of slaves, probably from Virginia, going to the market to be sold.
>
> Columbus, like so many towns on the borders of the granitic and tertiary regions, is situated at the head of the navigation of a large river, and the rapids of the Chatahoochie are well seen from the bridge by which it is here spanned. The vertical rise and fall of this river, which divides Georgia and Alabama, amounts to no less than sixty or seventy feet in the course of the year; and the geologist should visit the country in November, when the season is healthy, and the river low, for then he may see exposed to view, not only the horizontal tertiary strata, but the subjacent cretaceous deposits, containing

ammonites, baculites, and other characteristic fossils. These organic remains are met with some miles below the town, at a point called "Snake's Shoals;" and Dr. Boykin showed us a collection of the fossils, at his agreeable villa in the suburbs. In an excursion which I made with Mr. Pond to the Upotoy [Upatoi] Creek, I ascertained that the cretaceous beds are overlaid everywhere by tertiary strata, containing fossil wood and marine shells.[98]

The last detachment of Indians, a party of no less than 500, quitted Columbus only a week ago for Arkansas, a memorable event in the history of the settlement of this region, and part of an extensive and systematic scheme steadily pursued by the Government, of transferring the Aborigines from the Eastern States to the Far-West . . .[99]

The water-power at the rapids has been recently applied to some newly-erected cotton mills, and already an anti-free-trade party is beginning to be formed. The masters of these factories hope, by excluding coloured men-or, in other words, slaves- from all participation in the business, to render it a genteel employment for white operatives; a measure which places it in a strong light the inconsistencies entailed upon a community by slavery and the antagonism of races, for there are numbers of coloured mechanics in all these Southern States very expert at trades requiring much more skill and knowledge than the functions of ordinary work-people in factories. Several New Englanders, indeed, who have come from North to South Carolina and Georgia, complain to me that they cannot push on their children here, as carpenters, cabinet-makers, blacksmiths, and in other such crafts, because the planters bring up the most intelligent of their slaves to these occupations. The landlord of an inn confessed to me, that, being a carrier, he felt himself obliged to have various kinds of work done by coloured artisans, because they were the slaves of planters who employed him in his own line. "They interfere," said he, "with the fair competition of white mechanics, by whom I could have got the work better done."

These Northern settlers are compelled to preserve a discreet silence about such grievances when in the society of Southern slave-owners, but are open and eloquent in decanting upon them to a stranger. They are struck with the difficulty experienced in raising money here, by small shares, for the building of mills. "Why," say they, "should all our cotton make so long a journey to the North, to be manufactured there, and come back to us at so high a price? It is because all spare cash is sunk here in purchasing negroes. In order to get a week's work done for you, you must buy a negro out and out for life."

From Columbus we travelled fifty-five miles west to Chehaw, to join a railway, which was to carry us on to Montgomery . . .[100]

Typical American stagecoach of the type used by travelers visiting antebellum Columbus. *(From Basil Hall) Collection of the Columbus Museum, Columbus, Georgia; Museum purchase made possible by the Evelyn S. and H. Wayne Patterson Fund G. 2007.14. Courtesy of the Columbus Museum.*

→ 16 ←

ALEXANDER MACKAY, 1847

"We were so often threatened with an upset, that I at last came almost to wish for one, that, on this score at least, we might be relieved from our anxiety"

Alexander Mackay's account of a visit to Columbus barely mentions the city at all. Instead, he seems absorbed with the multiple troubles he encountered incident to his travels. His experiences were far from unique, however, as simply getting to the town offered many travelers as much drama as a stay. Area roads that appeared mere paths in the woods at the time of Columbus's founding had, in many instances, scarcely improved by the late 1840s, and at times wagon-rutted, mud-pitted, and haphazardly maintained roads were all but impassable throughout the town's antebellum years. Mackay's account reveals graphically—even comically—the very real difficulties associated with getting to Columbus in its early years.

A native of Scotland, Mackay was a career journalist with a burning curiosity about American society and abundant experience in writing about what he saw for his readers. It was through his work covering the Congressional debates over the signing of the Oregon Treaty (ownership of the Oregon Country had been contested between Britain and America for years before the compact officially divided the territory between the two countries) for the *London Morning Chronicle* that he visited the Chattahoochee Valley. Growing restless after an extended stay in the nation's capital, Mackay was determined to take advantage of his time in America by visiting as much of the country as he could. He ended up venturing through much of the South, up the Mississippi River, and into the Great Lakes area before making his return. In *Travels in the Western World*, which he published as a record of his journey, Mackay produced a wide-ranging documentary of the growing nation during a period of relative prosperity. The portrait he painted is of a dynamic, expanding, and modern nation incongruously vexed by slavery:[101]

> As we receded from Macon, the surface of the country began to improve a little, but not the condition of the roads. An additional quantity of rain had fallen during the night, with which the heavy clay was so churned up, that sometimes it was a marvel to me how we made any progress at all. On, however, we went at a painfully slow rate, sometimes stuck fast for a minute or two, then released by the horses, after they had been accorded a little breathing time; sometimes kept dancing between seat and roof, and at others reeling for minutes at a time from side to side. One of the frightful jolts which we every now and then experienced, caused me to receive a severe blow in the cheek from the side of the coach, which left its ugly mark upon me for some days afterwards. We were so often threatened with an upset, that I at last came almost to wish for one, that, on this score at least, we might be relieved from our anxiety. It was not long ere I was gratified. Giving a tremendous lurch to the side at which I was seated, the coach seemed for a moment to poise itself upon the two side wheels, as if deliberating whether to lie down at once or restore itself to its equilibrium. I looked at the judge, and shuddered at the idea of the "fourteen stun"; so, pressing towards the left, I called upon the rest to lean to the weather side. This they did but too effectually, for, on the coach righting, the opposite wheels plunged into another hole, or "rut," with such violence as to carry over the whole concern. It went gently enough, and I felt an inward satisfaction, as we were falling, that my weight was to come on the judge. I regretted it afterwards, on account of the rather severe contusions which together we occasioned to the commissioner.
>
> For a moment after the vehicle was fairly on its side there was neither motion nor sound within, every one seeming to be collecting his thoughts, and assuring himself precisely where and how he was. At length, the lady

in the back seat found courage to scream, which seemed to bring it to the recollection of the rest that there was something to be done as well for themselves as for others. There was accordingly a general movement of arms and legs; at least, of as many as were in a position to move; an operation which, unless checked, might have led to rather serious results, as heads and heels were in awkward juxtaposition. At one time, the iron nails in the shoe of one of those who, but a little before, had been occupying the front seat, gleamed ominously before my eyes, causing me to remove my head without delay as far as I could from the awkward apparition . . .

As we approached Columbus, the surface of the country became much more broken and picturesque than I had seen it at any point since leaving the coast . . . Columbus is but a small town, and is prettily situated on the east bank of the Chatahouchee, a navigable tributary of the Apalachicola, which empties itself into the Gulf of Mexico, close to the peninsula of Florida. Like Macon, though far inland, it has thus a navigable channel to the sea. It is the frontier town of Georgia, on the west, the Chatahouchee here separating that State from Alabama. There are some pretty falls and cataracts in the neighborhood of the town, which well repay the trouble of a visit . . .

President James Knox Polk. *Courtesy of the Library of Congress.*

→ 17 ←

PRESIDENT JAMES KNOX POLK, 1849

"My reception at Columbus was warm and cordial and every possible mark of respect was paid to me"

Only a month after leaving office following a busy term in the spring of 1849, did President James K. Polk visit Columbus as part of a Southern "good will" tour. Remembered in history as the first successful "dark horse" candidate for the presidency, the lawyer, congressman, and governor of Tennessee emerged from relative obscurity to win the nation's highest office. An outspoken expansionist, Polk had been consumed with a robust program of territorial acquisition during his presidency, becoming involved in acrimonious debate over Oregon and Mexico and ending up embroiled in war and political intrigue that resulted in the United States acquiring huge swaths of land in the Southwest and along the Pacific coast. Under his leadership, Manifest Destiny—the belief that the United States would ultimately and naturally stretch across the North American continent—became a reality. At the time, Polk was the youngest man to hold the presidency, and his energetic nationalism, Southern roots, and support of the rights of slaveholders made him supremely popular in the South.[102]

Accordingly, Columbus rolled out the red carpet for his arrival. Polk's brief visit reveals much about the community's status and wherewithal to entertain lavishly. The president's stay also shows clearly that Columbus was no longer a frontier backwater by any measure. The city had become wealthy and influential, with residents prominent on the national scene and capable of giving a warm welcome to dignitaries on par with that offered anywhere in the South. Traveling south through central Georgia and heading west at Macon, he stayed at a plantation owner's home just outside of town the evening before he arrived in the city. There, nearly two dozen citizens of Columbus, headed by leading light Seaborn Jones, greeted him to escort him into town.[103]

While Polk's account mentions a few individuals and locations by name, it is admittedly short on details. It is the visit itself, however, and the perfunctory treatment in the memoir of one of the most well-traveled men in America at that time, that are most revealing. Polk's account begins Thursday, 15 March 1849:

> After breakfast this morning we proceeded on our journey towards Columbus, a distance of about 20 miles, accompanied by the committee who had met us at Gen'l Lowe's last evening. On arriving within a mile of town we were met by the Mayor (who was a Whig in politics) and aldermen, and a large number of citizens in carriages and on horseback. I alighted from the carriage and was received by the Mayor, who made a short address to me to which I made a short reply. I was then introduced to the aldermen, and proceeded in an open carriage to the town. The procession passed through the principal streets, which were crowded with people, to the Court House, which is situated in a large open square. I was conducted to the upper porch of the Court House, on the 2nd floor, and in full view of several thousand persons who were assembled in the Court Yard below. I was addressed by the Hon. Seaborn Jones and responded to him. I was then conducted into a large Court room where hundreds of the people, male and female, were presented to me and with whom I shook hands. From this place I was conducted back to the carriage and was taken to the residence of the Hon. Walter T. Colquitt, late a Senator in Congress, who had invited me and my family to take lodgings in his hospitable mansion. About 4 o'clock, accompanied by Mr. Colquitt and the several members of the Committee, I attended a public Dinner prepared at a Hotel, of which a large company partook. After the cloth was removed a sentiment complimentary to me was given to which I replied in a short speech. After dinner I returned to the House of Judge Colquitt where I was introduced to a number of ladies and gentlemen of the

City. About 9 o'clock I was conducted by a committee to a splendid public Ball, and after partaking of a very fine supper returned to Judge Colquitt's House about 12 o'clock at night. Mrs. Polk, Miss Hays, and Miss Rucker, accompanied by Mrs. Colquitt, attended the Ball. The rain fell in torrents during the afternoon and night, and in going to and returning from the Ball the ladies and myself in carriages were exposed and became somewhat wet. My reception at Columbus was warm and cordial and every possible mark of respect was paid to me which I could desire. At the close of the labours of the day I was greatly wearied and worn down, and was heartily rejoiced when I had an opportunity to retire to rest. . .[104]

Frederick Law Olmsted. *Courtesy of the Library of Congress.*

18

FREDERICK LAW OLMSTED, 1853

"I had seen in no place . . ., so much gambling, intoxication, and cruel treatment of servants in public, as in Columbus"

Long before he became famous as the visionary designer of New York's Central Park and celebrated as the "father of landscape architecture," Frederick Law Olmsted visited Columbus as a quiet observer of culture. In his younger years, then-journalist and sometime social critic Olmsted ventured to western Georgia during a period of extensive travel that he later remarked on at length was "most interesting, amusing, and instructive." Restlessly exploring both the world and himself during these journeys, Olmstead used his experiences to write a lengthy list of articles that eventually formed the core of his acclaimed series of books providing commentary on life in the South.[105]

In *A Journey in the Seaboard Slave States with Remarks on Their Economy,* regarded by many as the seminal volume of his travel writing, Olmsted offered his thoughts on his 1853 stay in Columbus. While the stay at "several days" was relatively extended, his remarks about the town are very brief. Terse may actually be a more accurate description of the account, as Olmsted apparently held the town in low regard for its rough manners and crude accommodations. There were notable exceptions, he acknowledged, but overall the three paragraphs devoted to describing Columbus demonstrate that even as the emerging industrial hub was coming into its own it remained plagued by a variety of ills. Some of those are era-specific—slavery foremost—and some are the timeless complaints of discriminating travelers.[106]

At Columbus, I spent several days. It is the largest manufacturing town, south of Richmond, in the Slave States. It is situated at the Falls, and the head of steamboat navigation of the Chattahoochee, the western boundary of Georgia. The water-power is sufficient to drive two hundred thousand spindles, with a proportionate number of looms. There are, probably, at present from fifteen to twenty thousand spindles running. The operatives in the cotton-mills are said to be mainly "Cracker girls" (poor whites from the country), who earn, in good times, by piece-work, from $8 to $12 a month. There are, besides, the cotton-mills, one woolen-mill, one paper-mill, a foundry, a cotton-gin factory, a machine-shop, etc. The labourers in all these are mainly whites, and they are in such a condition that, if temporarily thrown out of employment, great numbers of them are at once reduced to a state of destitution, and are dependent upon credit or charity for their daily food. Public entertainments were being held at the time of my visit, the profits to be applied to the relief of operatives in mills which had been stopped by the effects of a late flood of the river. Yet Slavery is constantly boasted to be a perfect safeguard against such distress.

I had seen in no place, since I left Washington, so much gambling, intoxication, and cruel treatment of servants in public, as in Columbus. This, possibly, was accidental; but I must caution persons, travelling for health or pleasure, to avoid stopping in the town. The hotel in which I lodged was disgustingly dirty; the table revolting; the waiters stupid, inattentive, and annoying. It was the stage-house; but I was informed that the other public-house was no better. There are very good inns at Macon, and at Montgomery, Alabama; and it will be best for an invalid proceeding from Savannah westward, if possible, not to spend a night between these towns.

I should add that I met with much courtesy from strangers, and saw as much real hospitality of disposition among the people near Columbus, as anywhere else in the South. I was much gratified by a visit to the garden of Mr. Peabody, a horticulturist, who has succeeded wonderfully in cultivation strawberries upon a poor, sandy soil, in a climate of great heat and dryness, by a thin mulching of leaves.[107]

→ EPILOGUE ←

The Columbus Frederick Law Olmsted visited was not so much a city on the make as one on the cusp of its antebellum zenith, unaware of how soon it would be ushering in a new era. In the city's twenty-fifth year of existence, it could lay claim to a population of six thousand people and had become the economic, social, political, and transportation hub of a relatively wealthy and growing region. Change was in the air, however. Much of what antebellum Columbus strove to be, like most of the South, lay bound up in a societal system soon destined to come to an end. By the time Olmsted came through town, people everywhere were keenly aware of a looming showdown over the issue of slavery that could unravel the intertwined strings of commerce and culture that tied the region so tightly together. While most hoped the contest that would ultimately decide the perpetual question regarding the place of the institution within the nation would be strictly political, increasingly it became clear that many in the South were willing to take up arms to defend their position on the matter. Columbus proved to be no exception, and as much as any location, the city became caught up in the mounting crisis in the years after Olmsted's departure. The possibility of war and its ramifications hovered over public and private discourse for years prior to the event and, in general, steadily became part of the tenor of life in the city long before shots were fired.

During the war that eventually erupted in 1861, Columbus served as an important nexus for a variety of wartime activities. In addition to sending hundreds of men to the front, the city became one of the Confederacy's preeminent military-industrial complexes, supplying an incredible range of munitions and material to the fledgling war-born and war-torn nation. During these chaotic years, Columbus's population swelled to nearly double its prewar high, as refugees and the unemployed fled to its relative security and opportunity far behind the front lines of the conflict. Five springs bloomed on the banks of the Chattahoochee before shots finally were fired in a military contest for Columbus, and those came so late in the war that, in hindsight, it seems pointless. Nevertheless, the local chapter of the city's national drama came to a devastating finale in April 1865 with a destructive raid that in local memory officially marked the end of the war. The entire conflict, from Fort Sumter to Appomattox, came to be understood as one long watershed event that cleanly demarcated all that came before from all that came after—not only in Columbus, but across the South.

Reality, of course, is not so neat. If we filter the story carefully, equal strains of persistence and incremental change are evident and better describe the history of antebellum and postwar Columbus than any sudden epiphany that a new era had dawned with the departure of Union General James H. Wilson's raiders. Enough real changes nevertheless took place that the old shibboleth still works. The war devastated Columbus. It left the economy in ruins, hundreds of people homeless, even more families broken and grieving, and much of its industrial core in ashes. More significantly, it fundamentally altered the nature of the society in which the city was born, nurtured, and flourished by destroying the institution of slavery. The city would wrestle with these repercussions for years, decades, and more.

Columbus eventually made a fuller economic recovery from the war than many of its peer cities, heralding another coming of age in which its population boomed and its factories redoubled their size and influence. The city outgrew the original plan, so carefully plotted by its designer, expanding primarily north and east before the original core ultimately became so tangential to the city's sprawl that it was overlooked and largely forgotten. Save for the framework on which the city was erected, most of what was there when Olmsted visited has been lost the ravages of time and growth. Today, though, the original city is the focus of renewed vitality as Columbus reorients itself toward the river and proactively works to make downtown a cultural, educational, and economic center for a diverse and growing modern community. It is exactly the type of vibrancy the city's founders envisioned for those 1,200 acres on the eastern bank of the Chattahoochee and exactly the type of activity—even if the sights and sounds have changed—that antebellum visitors experienced.

TOUR OF HISTORIC SITES

This tour of historic sites associated with antebellum Columbus is designed to show readers how the early town may have looked to visitors. Included here are selected structures dating to the antebellum era, as well as several sites where community landmarks of the era once stood. It includes only those sites lying within, or closely associated, with the original town of Columbus as surveyed by Edward Lloyd Thomas, an area of some 1,200 acres bordered by the Chattahoochee River on the west, Sixteenth Street at the north, Highway 280 (Fourth Street) in the south, and Sixth Avenue in the east. It encompasses an area approximately a mile and a half from north to south and about three quarters of a mile wide. To the north, south, and east of the original city of Columbus lay "commons"—areas reserved for community use; the riverbank on the city's western border was originally to be held out for public use as well. Though closely connected with the civic, social, and economic life of the early city, the several large antebellum estates constructed north and east of town that still stand, such as Dinglewood, St. Elmo, The Cedars, and The Elms, are beyond the scope of this book.

The original town plan is largely intact, and most of the city's streets are still accessible. There are some exceptions. Several blocks of the northwestern quadrant of Thomas's town plan, primarily in the area of Fifteenth and Sixteenth streets, are now occupied by the campus of Total Systems Services (TSYS). Also, portions of Bay Street, the modern street closest to the river, have been lost to development. Short Street, which ran along the river bluff between Eighth and Tenth streets in the area of current Woodruff Riverfront Park and the Columbus Convention and Trade Center, no longer exists as well. Also gone is one of the city's most unusual streets, created in 1837 by a group of local businessmen headed by John Warren. Running diagonally between Broadway and Fourteenth Street, Warren Street, alternately known as "Triangle Street" or even "Dog Alley," was obliterated during construction of the downtown branch of the YMCA several years ago.

The landscape of the original city is a relatively flat plain on the eastern bank of the Chattahoochee River. The area slopes gently from north to south, and to the east an abrupt line of hills rise. At the time of Columbus's founding, the area lay covered with a variety of ancient pine and hardwoods, with several small swamps and ponds, particularly in its eastern extremities.

DRIVING TOUR

This driving tour will take you past some of the most prominent sites in antebellum Columbus, and allow you to see a large portion of the city's remaining antebellum structures. The optional sites to visit, a list of which is included below, are destinations in their own right and require more than a drive-by visit to appreciate. They each feature nearby or on-site parking.

✻ Start at the **Columbus Convention and Visitor's Bureau (CVB) (900 Front Avenue)**. Take a right out of the parking lot onto Broadway, and then turn right onto Ninth Street. The Columbus CVB is housed in a historic downtown warehouse building.

1 On the left will be the **Columbus Marriott Hotel (800 Front Avenue)**. Portions of this modern hotel include elements of the old E. T. Taylor Cotton Gin manufactory (1847) and the Empire Mills facility (1861), founded by prominent industrialist George Woodruff. The mill was spared destruction during the Civil War because of its importance in producing food for the community. By the 1880s, it was the largest meal and flour mill in the South.

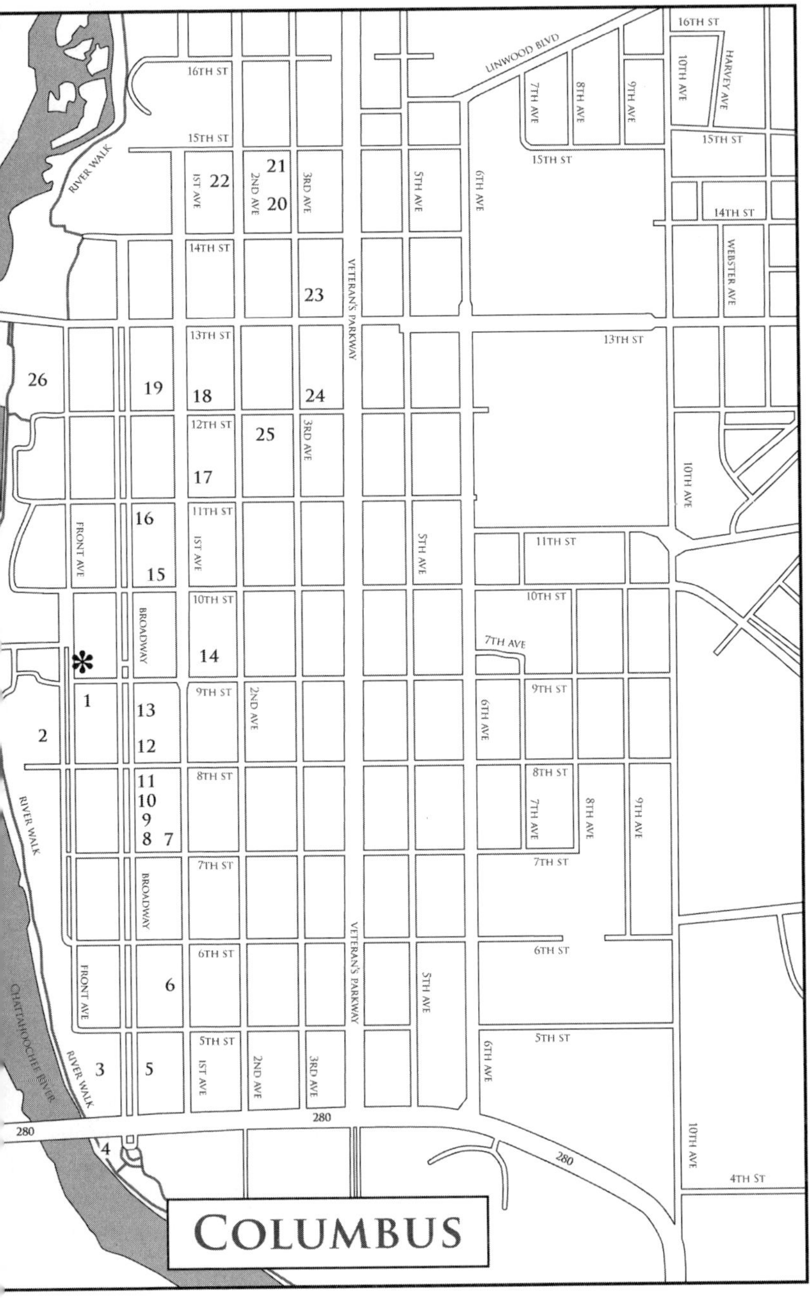
COLUMBUS
16TH ST
15TH ST
14TH ST
13TH ST
12TH ST
11TH ST
10TH ST
9TH ST
8TH ST
7TH ST
6TH ST
5TH ST
4TH ST
LINWOOD BLVD
1ST AVE
2ND AVE
3RD AVE
5TH AVE
6TH AVE
7TH AVE
8TH AVE
9TH AVE
10TH AVE
HARVEY AVE
WEBSTER AVE
VETERAN'S PARKWAY
FRONT AVE
BROADWAY
RIVER WALK
CHATTAHOOCHEE RIVER
280
1
2
3
4
5
6
7
8
9
10
11
12
13
14
15
16
17
18
19
20
21
22
23
24
25
26
*

2 Take a left onto Front Avenue. On the right will be the **Columbus Ironworks (801 Front Avenue)**. Established in 1853 by early Columbus industrialist William R. Brown, the Columbus Ironworks eventually grew into one of the city's most important manufacturing concerns. In its early years it produced a wide variety of items such as kettles, sugar, grist and saw mills, steam engines, and cotton gins. During the Civil War, the facility underwent major expansion as the Confederate Naval Iron Works. Most of the current facility, which is now operated as a convention and trade center, dates to the early 1900s.

3 Take a left onto Sixth Street, go one block, then turn right onto Broadway. After you pass Fifth Street, on the right will be the **Goetchius House (405 Broadway)**. Originally located at the corner of Second Avenue and Eleventh Street, this house was built in 1839 by architect Richard Rose Goetchius as a wedding gift for his wife, Mary Anne Bennett. Goetchius moved to Columbus from New York in 1834. The design of the home was inspired by the architecture of the elegant houses in New Orleans. It is the only home in the original city to feature such architecture. The home was moved to this location around 1970 and has served as a restaurant and special event center since that time.

4 Continue to the end of Broadway, driving under the Oglethorpe Bridge. You will be overlooking South Commons and the **site of Kennard's (Kinnard's) Ferry**. A small settlement featuring three or four trading houses, a tavern, ferry

operation, and a few houses occupied the riverbank just below here at the time of Columbus's founding. Known alternately as "Wewoka" or as "Kennard's Ferry" in honor of the Scottish-Yuchi family that operated the crossing and the tavern, the settlement sprang up on the north fork of the Federal Road, which crossed the river near this site. The community's exact origins are unclear, but date perhaps to as early as circa 1820. By viewing the river from the south end of Broadway, you can see the general vicinity of the ferry below. Most of the settlement probably would have been located in what is now South Commons.

5 Head back up Broadway. In the first block on the right, opposite of the Goetchius House, is the **Old Holy Family Catholic Church Rectory (412 Broadway)**. Constructed in 1835 to serve Columbus's first Catholic church, the St. Philip and James Parish (on what is now Chapel Street), this house was moved from the northeast corner of Seventh Street and Second Avenue in 1976.

6 Continue on Broadway to Fifth Street and turn right. Continue one block and take a left onto First Avenue. On the left will be **The Folly (527 First Avenue)**. This unusual octagon-shaped house is a National Historic Landmark. The home began as an early 1830s simple frame home. It was the home of US

Senator and Congressman Alfred Iverson and his wife Julia Forsyth, daughter of Georgia Governor John Forsyth. In 1863, local contractor Leander May remodeled it into the octagonal style made popular by author, lecturer, and health advocate Orson Squire Fowler. It reputedly is the only double octagonal home in the United States.

7 Continue to Seventh Street and take a left. On the right will be the **King-Barker House (13 Seventh Street)**. One of the few original Federal-style structures in the original city of Columbus, this home was built in 1835. It has undergone substantial modification.

8 Next door is the **Pemberton House (11 Seventh Street).** John Stith Pemberton, inventor of the formula for Coca-Cola, lived in this home from 1855 to 1860. It was originally located on Third Avenue, and moved to this site in the 1970s. Pemberton moved to Columbus in 1853 to practice pharmacy. He operated at least two drugstores in Columbus, and it was here that he first experimented with soda fountain drinks.

9 Take a right onto Broadway. On the right will be the **Woodruff Farm House (708 Broadway)**. Constructed around 1840, this house originally was located several miles east of Columbus. The Woodruff family used it as a summer residence later before donating it to the Historic Columbus Foundation. It was placed on this site in 1986. Behind the house is a circa 1810 **Trader's Cabin (708 ½ Broadway)**, which was moved here at the same time as the Woodruff Farm House. It is an excellent example of the type of cabin that would have been used by traders and early American settlers in this area around the time of the founding of Columbus. It is considered to be the oldest standing structure in Muscogee County.

10 Next door is **Dr. Pemberton's Country Home (712 Broadway).** John S. Pemberton lived in this house from 1860 until he moved to Atlanta. During this time he is believed to have first formulated his "French Wine of Cocoa," which became the forerunner of Coca-Cola. During the Civil War, Pemberton served in the Confederate Cavalry and was wounded in the Battle of Columbus. Originally located a few miles north of here, this home was moved to this site in 1977 so that it could be included in the Columbus Historic District.

11 Next door is the **Walker-Peters-Langdon House (716 Broadway).** Reputed to be the oldest house in the original city of Columbus, the Walkers-Peters-Langdon House dates to Columbus's founding in 1828. The Federal-style cottage stands on one of the original lots surveyed in Edward Lloyd Thomas's town plan. Records show that Colonel Virgil Walker purchased the lot, but the Nathaniel Peters family may have been the first to occupy the home. Behind the house is a **slave cabin** that was moved here from behind a house that once stood in the 1300 block of Second Avenue. Though individual circumstances varied greatly, the structure is typical of the type of housing provided for bondsmen in the antebellum Columbus area.

12 Continue on Broadway past Eighth Street. The second house on the right is the **Thomas-Kivline-Wolhwender House (808 Broadway).** A portion of this house is reputed to be the home in which Edward Lloyd Thomas's son Truman was carried to when he fell ill during the survey for the city and died on March 28, 1828. The small original structure was incorporated into a larger home later and underwent significant remodeling in the late 1800s.

13 A few doors down is the **Joseph House (828 Broadway)**. The Joseph House was built around 1842. It is most closely associated with the family of steamboat owner Isaac Joseph, whose family occupied the home for over century beginning in the 1860s. Originally built as a Greek Revival Cottage, it later received modification with Victorian elements.

14 Take a right onto Ninth Street. Go one block, and take a left onto First Avenue. On the right, where the Columbus Consolidated Government Center stands, is the **site of Muscogee County Courthouse (100 Tenth Street)**. This location has been the home of Columbus courthouses for nearly two centuries. The original survey of

Columbus tentatively reserved a space in the northern portion of the city, bounded by what is now Fifteenth and Sixteenth streets and First and Second avenues, for a county courthouse, but it was never utilized for that purpose. The first county courthouse, a simple wooden structure built shortly after the city's founding, stood a short distance from this location on First Avenue. A brick structure located at this site replaced it in 1838. It stood until the 1890s. The third courthouse stood on this site until the completion of the current government center in 1972.

15 Take a left onto Tenth Street. On the right, on the site occupied by Columbus State University's Rankin Center, is the **site of the Columbus Hotel**. The entire block, stretching along Tenth Street from First Avenue to Broadway, has been an

important commercial center continuously since Columbus's founding. The lot at the corner of Tenth Street and Broadway was reputedly the single most valuable lot in the original auction of lots in the city of Columbus. The Columbus Hotel was built on this spot, later succeeded by the antebellum Cook's Hotel, renamed the Rankin Hotel during the Civil War. Burned in 1878, the Rankin was rebuilt in 1880 and operated until 1972. The Rankin Center incorporates parts of the 1880s rebuilding of the Rankin Hotel as well as earlier structures in the block.

16 Turn right onto Broadway and continue to the intersection with Eleventh Street. On the corner is the **"Iron Bank" Building (6 West Eleventh Street)**. This building was constructed as the headquarters office of the Georgia Home Company. Work began in the late 1850s, with completion taking place after the Civil War. Its unusual façade is made of prefabricated cast iron, believed to have been shipped from Pittsburgh before the outbreak of the Civil War. Local, unsubstantiated legend holds that during the war, millions of dollars worth of Confederate gold were sent to Columbus from New Orleans before that city's capture and stored in the vault of the building by Bank of Columbus president William H. Young.

17 Take a right onto Eleventh Street, then turn left onto First Avenue. On the right will be **First Presbyterian Church (1100 First Avenue)**. Founded in 1830, the church moved to this location in 1862 when the sanctuary here was built. The church has undergone multiple expansions over the years.

18 Continue north on First Avenue. As you cross Twelfth Street, on the right is the Flowers Building, **site of the Oglethorpe House Hotel (1204 First Avenue)**. Here stood one of antebellum Columbus's premier hospitality establishments. The structure was built in 1836. It hosted Presidents James K. Polk and Millard Fillmore and noted American political figure Henry Clay on their visits here. During the Second Creek War, General Winfield Scott set up his headquarters here.

19 On the left, in the area today occupied by a parking lot, is the **site of Temperance Hall**. Three stories tall and one hundred feet long, Temperance Hall was the largest building in antebellum Columbus. Its cornerstone was laid in 1849. It served as a multi-purpose entertainment center in its early years, and hosted many community events such as plays and performances and became the location for special celebrations such as the reception of prominent dignitaries. During the Civil War, it served as a Confederate hospital.

20 Continue on First Avenue to Fourteenth Street and turn right. Go one block and turn left onto Second Avenue. About halfway down the block on the right will be the **Illges House (1428 Second Avenue)**. Built circa 1850 by James A. Chapman, the house is a reminder

of the grand homes that once stood in this area of Columbus, known locally as "High Uptown." The home is Greek Revival in style but features Italianate alterations added in the 1870s. It features six massive Corinthian columns across its front. Last used as a residence several decades ago, the home has been converted into office space.

21 Next door is the **Rankin House (1440 Second Avenue)**. The home serves as the headquarters of Historic Columbus, which maintains it as an office and house museum. It also houses the organization's research library. The home was built for Scottish immigrant James Rankin, owner of the Rankin Hotel. Work began on the house before the Civil War, but was not completed until afterwards. The fence surrounding the property formerly bordered the upper Broadway townhouse of General Henry Lewis Benning, namesake of Fort Benning.

22 Opposite the Rankin House on Second Avenue are the **McGehee-Woodall House (1443 Second Avenue)** and the **Schley-Peabody-Swift-Warner House (1445 Second Avenue)**. Built circa 1845 for Robert Alexander, the McGehee-Woodall house most closely is associated with later owners, especially A. C. McGehee. A noted businessman during the antebellum era, McGehee ran a slave trading operation in Columbus with a partner for several years and was a part owner of the slave ship *Wanderer*, one of the last documented ships to bring African slaves to the

United States (1858). The home has served a variety of uses over its long history; it was most recently utilized as a senior citizens' center. The Schley-Peabody-Swift-Warner House was built circa 1840 by Philip Thomas Schley, an officer in the local militia unit the Muscogee Blues. The home originally stood on the site of First Presbyterian Church (1100 First Avenue) and was moved to this location in 1858. Prominent American philanthropist George Foster Peabody lived here as a child with his family during the Civil War. Later, the Swift family and former Confederate Naval Ironworks Chief Engineer James H. Warner occupied the home.

23 Turn right onto Fifteenth Street, go one block, and turn right onto Third Avenue. About halfway down the next block on the left is **The Lion House (Hoxey-Cargill House, 1316 Third Avenue)**. Popularly known for the pair of iron castings at its entrance, the house is believed to date to the late 1840s. The home was built by prominent resident Thomas Hoxey, organizer of the Columbus Lyceum, and reputedly designed by nationally known Philadelphia architect Stephen Decatur Button.

24 Proceed on Third Avenue to the intersection with Twelfth Street. On the left is the **Swift-Kyle House (303 Twelfth Street)**. Built just before the outbreak of the Civil War, the Swift-Kyle House has had several owners. It is most closely associated with its postwar occupation by textile industry magnate George Parker Swift and his son in law James P. Kyle. Local tradition holds that Union troops occupied it after the Battle of Columbus in April of 1865.

25 Turn right onto Twelfth Street. On the left is **First Baptist Church (212 Twelfth Street)**. First Baptist Church traces its origins to a meeting of a dozen men and women on Broad Street in 1829 who organized the city's first Baptist congregation. As the northern half of this block had been reserved for use by religious institutions in the survey for Columbus, the group constructed a church here in 1830. It was replaced by a larger structure in 1840. The current sanctuary was built in 1859, making it the only house of worship that dates to the antebellum era standing on one of the lots reserved for churches in the original town survey.

26 Continue three blocks on Twelfth Street to the intersection with Front Avenue. Ahead and to the right, stretching the full block between Twelfth and Thirteenth Streets, is the Eagle and Phenix Mills complex, **site of Eagle Mill (1201 Front Avenue)**. Eagle Mill, forerunner of the sprawling industrial complex known as the Eagle and Phenix Mills, stood on this site. Prominent industrialist William H. Young built the original facility, one of antebellum Columbus's largest employers, here in 1851. Destroyed during the Civil War, it was rebuilt and underwent went multiple expansions to become one of the largest mill facilities in the South.

Turn left onto Front Avenue and return to the Columbus Convention and Visitor's Bureau (900 Front Avenue) or visit some of the sites listed below, which are best viewed on foot.

OPTIONAL TOUR SITES

A **Chattahoochee Riverwalk (multiple points of entry along Front and Bay Avenue and also at Fourteenth Street):** The Chattahoochee Riverwalk parallels the river as it forms the western and southern boundary of the original city of Columbus. Offering scenic views of the river, it is

accessible to hikers and bikers through multiple points of entry. Strolling along the riverwalk roughly between the Fourteenth and Dillingham street bridges will take one past the sites of most of the "water lots," which were auctioned off by the city for the development of water-powered industry. This early industrial development, harnessing the abundant power of the Chattahoochee, significantly contributed to Columbus's unique identity as a Deep South industrial town. Behind the Columbus Ironworks along the riverwalk is the **site of Columbus Wharf**. The primary landing for steamboats docking at Columbus for more than one hundred years, the wharf was long a major landmark in the city. The site acted as a nerve center for trade in the city's early years, constantly buzzing with the activity of stevedores loading and unloading cotton and a wide variety of goods and passengers boarding and disembarking. The site of the "boatyard," where the few steamboats built in antebellum Columbus were constructed, lies just south of the wharf, in the vicinity of the amphitheater adjacent to the Chattahoochee Riverwalk in the area between Sixth and Seventh streets.

B **City Mills (1 Eighteenth Street):** The oldest manufacturing establishment on the river in Columbus, City Mills began operation just north of the original town limit the year of the city's founding. Prominent early resident Seaborn Jones built the grist mill on Lot No. 1 in the "Coweta Falls reserve" in which Columbus was located. Milling operations continued here for more than 150 years. The brick structure that stands on the site today, currently abandoned, replaced the original wooden facility.

C **Linwood Cemetery (721 Linwood Boulevard):** Linwood Cemetery is the oldest cemetery in Columbus, tracing its beginning to the founding of the city in 1828. Truman Thomas, son of town planner Edward L. Thomas, died during the survey of the town and became the first person buried here. Numerous early Columbus settlers and their descendants are interred here. Notable graves include those of Coca-Cola inventor John S. Pemberton, General Henry L. Benning, first Columbus intendant Ulysses Lewis, founder of the Georgia Woman Suffrage Association Helen Augusta Howard, and more than two hundred Confederate soldiers.

D **Site of the Calhoun-Griffin-Mott House, Chattahoochee Riverwalk at Fourteenth Street:** Built in 1841 by James S. Calhoun, the Calhoun-Griffin-Mott House was the last surviving grand home that once fronted the Chattahoochee. The house was occupied by Daniel Griffin, president of the Southern Telegraph Line, in the 1850s. He sold it to Randolph Mott in 1856. Union General James H. Wilson made his headquarters here after the Battle of Columbus in 1865. A staunch Unionist, Mott alleged the home "had never left the Union." The home was irreparably damaged by a fire in 2014.

E **Porterdale Cemetery (107 Tenth Avenue):** Porterdale Cemetery sits on land that was originally part of the South

Commons reserve in the original town plan for Columbus. The earliest known grave is 1836, but some of the unmarked graves may predate this burial. The cemetery traces its origins to the

black cemetery in the original town plan that was presumably the burial ground for many antebellum Columbus slaves. The cemetery is believed to be named after the first African-American sexton in Columbus, Richard Porter. Among the notable figures buried here is Columbus singer Gertrude "Ma" Rainey, known as the "Mother of the Blues."

F **Old Slave Cemetery (600 block of East Sixth Street):** The original town plan for Columbus indicates that a cemetery for black residents was located on the east side of Sixth Avenue between Sixth and Seventh streets. Although not confirmed by archaeology, local tradition holds that burials for blacks were held here in the city's early years. Once bisected by a railroad, the lot is otherwise largely undeveloped. A portion of it is included in the "Resting Garden," which commemorates the site's significance in local African-American history.

G **Dillingham Street Bridge:** The modern concrete span crossing the Chattahoochee at Dillingham Street stands on the site of an original covered bridge built in 1838. First known as the "Columbus Bridge," and later as the "Lower Bridge" after the construction of the bridge at Franklin (Fourteenth) Street, the original structure was built by noted slave craftsman Horace King. Traveling over the Columbus Bridge, many antebellum visitors would have continued their journey westward.

H **South Commons (access via Fourth Avenue/Highway 27):** One of three original common areas set aside for community use in the original town plan, South Commons continues to serve its intended purpose. Today it is home to such community venues as Golden Park, A. J. McClung Memorial

Stadium, the Columbus Softball Complex, and the Columbus Civic Center. In the antebellum era, it was the location of a community hospital, known as the "pesthouse," and a horse racing track that stood in the general area of Memorial Stadium.

Those interested in touring additional pre-Civil War historic sites within the boundaries of the original city of Columbus should visit three outdoor interpretive parks located in downtown Columbus. **Promenade Park**, which is located on the bluff between First Avenue and the Chattahoochee Riverwalk roughly between Fifth and Seventh streets offers scenic views of the Chattahoochee, and features several kiosks installed in the 1980s that interpret aspects of local history. A special "Founder's Area" of the park is located at the intersection of Fifth Street and Front Avenue. Nearby **Heritage Park**, located at Seventh Street between Front and Broad streets, honors the pioneering entrepreneurs and workers who transformed Columbus into an industrial and trading center. It features a series of outdoor sculptures interpreting the role of agriculture and the textile, gristmill, brick, and foundry industries. It also includes vignettes commemorating the importance of the river in regional development, and the local connection to Coca-Cola. **Woodruff Riverfront Park**, located adjacent to Bay Avenue between Eleventh Street and Dillingham Street, provides access to the Chattahoochee Riverwalk and allows viewing the scenic rapids of the river. In addition, there are some interpretive panels explaining the importance of the site to Native Americans and early Columbus development.

ANTEBELLUM COLUMBUS STREET-NAME GUIDE

(All roads were named "streets" in the original town plan.)

Current Street	Original Street Name
Fourth Street	Covington Street
Fifth	Fulton
Sixth	Early
Seventh	Few
Eighth	Baldwin
Ninth	Thomas
Tenth	Crawford
Eleventh	St. Clair
Twelfth	Randolph
Thirteenth	Bryan
Fourteenth	Franklin
Fifteenth	Bridge
Sixteenth	Washington

Current Avenues	Original Name
Bay	Bay
Front	Front
Broadway	Broad
First	Oglethorpe
Second	Jackson
Third	Troup
Fourth	Forsyth
Fifth	McIntosh
Sixth	Mercer

BIBLIOGRAPHY

Arfwedson, C. D. *The United States and Canada, in 1832, 1833, and 1834*. London: Richard Bentley, New Burlington Street, 1834.

Alabama Department of Archives and History

Autry, Dolores. *Historic Linwood Cemetery of Columbus, Muscogee County, GA*. Columbus, GA: N.p., 1992.

Benton, Jeffery C., ed. *The Very Worst Road: Travellers' Accounts of Crossing Alabama's Old Creek Indian Territory, 1820–1847*. Tuscaloosa: University of Alabama Press, 2009.

Borneman, Walter R. *Polk: The Man Who Transformed the Presidency and America*. New York: Random House, 2009.

Buckingham, James S. *The Slave States of America*. London: Fisher, Son and Co., 1842.

Bunn, Mike, and Doug Purcell. *Images of America: Lower Chattahoochee River*. Charleston, SC: Arcadia Press, 2007.

Burke, John. *The Royal Families of England, Scotland, and Wales, with Their Descendants, Sovereigns and Subject.* London: E. Churton, 1851.

Cadle, Farris W. *Georgia Land Surveying History and Law*. Athens: University of Georgia Press, 1991.

Carey, Anthony Gene. *Sold Down the River: Slavery in the Lower Chattahoochee Valley of Alabama and Georgia*. Tuscaloosa: University of Alabama Press, 2011.

Clark, Thomas D., ed. *Travels in the Old South: A Bibliography*, 3 vols. Norman: University of Oklahoma Press, 1956.

Cobb, James C. *Georgia Odyssey: A Short History of the State.* Athens: University of Georgia Press, 2008.

Coleman, Kenneth L., ed. *A History of Georgia.* Athens: University of Georgia Press, 1991.

The Columbus Museum

Columbus State University Archives, Historic Newspaper Collection

Columbus State University Archives (Historical Photograph Collection).

Cox, John. *Traveling South: Travel Narratives and the Construction of American Identity*. Athens: University of Georgia Press, 2005.

DeTreville, John R. "The Little New South: Origins of Industry in Georgia's Fall-Line Cities, 1840–1865." PhD diss., University of North Carolina Press, 1986.

Deaton, Mrs. John. *History of Medicine in Columbus, Ga., 1828–1971*. Columbus, GA: The Woman's Auxiliary of the Muscogee County Medical Society, 197? (unknown publication date).

Elliott, Rita Folse. *Living in Columbus, Georgia 1828–1869: The Lives of Creeks, Traders, Enslaved African Americans, Mill Operatives and Others as Told to Archaeologists*. Columbus, GA: City of Columbus, 2005.

Ellisor, John T. *The Second Creek War: Interethnic Conflict and Collusion on a Collapsing Frontier*. Lincoln: University of Nebraska Press, 2010.

Emory University Manuscript, Archives and Rare Books Library

Featherstonhaugh, George William. *Excursion Through the Slave States*. London: John Murray, 1844.

Galer, Mary Jane. *Columbus, Georgia Lists of People, 1828–1852 and Sexton's Reports to 1866*. Columbus, GA: Iberian Publishing Co., 2000.

Georgia Archives

Goff, John. "Edward Lloyd Thomas, Surveyor," *Emory University Quarterly* 18.2 (Summer 1962): 107–19.

Gilbert, James J. *A History of the First Presbyterian Church of Columbus, Georgia, During the First 100 Years of Its Existence*. Columbus, GA: Gilbert Printing Co., 1930.

Hall, Basil. *Travels in North America, in the Years 1827 and 1828*. Edinburgh, Scotland: Cadell and Co., 1829.

Harris, Roger. *Our Town: An Introduction to the History of Columbus, Georgia*. Columbus, GA: Historic Columbus Foundation, 1992.

Historic Columbus Foundation

Keller, Helen Barker. "The History of the Theater in Columbus, Georgia from 1828–1865." Master's thesis, University of Georgia, 1934.

Kilbourne, Elizabeth Evans. *Columbus, Georgia, Newspaper Clippings*. Savannah, GA: E.E. Kilbourne, 1997.

Knight, Lucian Lamar. *Reminiscences of Famous Georgians: Embracing Episodes and Incidents in the Lives of the Great Men of the State* (Ithaca, NY: Cornell University Library, 2009 [reprint]). First edition: Atlantic: Franklin-Turnes Company, 1908.

Kyle, F. Clason. *Images: A Pictorial History of Columbus, Georgia.* Norfolk, VA: Donning Co., 1986.

Kyle, F. Clason, and Lewis O. Powell. *In Order of Appearance: Chronicling 135 Years on America's Most Celebrated Stage.* Columbus, GA: Communicorp, 2006.

Lee, Sidney, ed. *Dictionary of National Biography: Index and Epitome*. London: Smith, Elder, and Co., 1903.

Library of Congress, Prints and Photographs Online Catalog. www.loc.gov/pictures.

Logan, Deborah Anna. *The Hour and the Woman: Harriet Martineau's "Somewhat Remarkable" Life*. Dekalb: Northern Illinois University Press, 2002.

Lupold, John. *Columbus, Georgia 1828–1978*. Columbus, GA: Columbus Sesquicentennial, 1978.

Lupold, John, and Thomas L. French, Jr. *Bridging Deep South Rivers: The Life and Legend of Horace King*. Athens: University of Georgia Press, 2004.

Lupold, John, Virginia Tucker Peebeles, Matthews Dismuke Swift, and Elizabeth Kelley Barker. *Heritage Park: A Celebration of the Industrial Heritage of Columbus, Georgia*. Columbus, GA: Historic Columbus Foundation, 1999.

Lyell, Charles. *A Second Visit to the United States of North America*. London: John Murray, 1849.

Mackay, Alexander. *The Western World: Travels in the United States in 1846–47*. London: Richard Bentley, 1849.

Mahan, Joseph B. *Columbus: Georgia's Fall Line Trading Town.* Northridge, CA: Windsor Publications, 1986.

Mahan, Katherine Hines. "History of Music in Columbus, Georgia, 1828–1928." PhD diss. Florida State University, 1968.

Mahan, Katherine Hines, and William C. Woodall. *A History of Public Education in Muscogee County and the City of Columbus, Georgia, 1828–1976*. Columbus, GA: Muscogee County Board of Education, 1977.

Mahan, Katherine Hines. *Showboats to Soft Shoes: A Century of Musical Development in Columbus, Georgia, 1828–1928*. Columbus, GA: Columbus Office Supply Co., 1968.

Martin, John H. *Columbus, Georgia, From Its Selection as a Trading Town in 1827, To Its Partial Destruction by Wilson's Raid in 1865*. Columbus, GA: Thomas Gilbert, 1874.

Martineau, Harriet. *Society in America*. Paris: Baudry's European Library, 1837.

Maxwell, Alice S., and Marion B. Dunlevy. *Virago! The Story of Anne Newport Royall*. Jefferson, NC: McFarland, Inc., 1985.

Minnesota Historical Society Collections Online Database

Moses, Montrose Jonas. *Famous Actor-Families in America*. New York: Thomas D. Crowell and Co., 1906.

Mueller, Edward A. *Perilous Journeys: A History of Steamboating on the Chattahoochee, Apalachicola, and Flint Rivers, 1828–1928*. Eufaula, AL: Historic Chattahoochee Commission, 1990.

O'Connell, Deirdre. *The Ballad of Blind Tom, Slave Pianist*. New York: Overlook Press, 2009.

Olmsted, Frederick Law. *A Journey in the Seaboard Slave States with Remarks on Their Economy,* New York: Dix and Edwards, 1856.

Peddy, Thomas Joseph. *Olden Days in Columbus, Georgia 1842–1856; As Described in Columns from the Columbus Enquirer-Sun During 1895–1898*. Columbus, GA: N.p., 1990.

Pope-Hennessy, Una. *The Aristocratic Journey: Being the Outspoken Letters of Mrs. Basil Hall Written during a Fourteen Months' Sojourn in America, 1827–1828*. New York: Knickerbocker Press, 1931.

Power, Tyrone. *Impression of America During the Years 1833, 1834, and 1835*. Philadelphia: Carey, Lea and Blanchard, 1836.

Quaife, Milo Milton, ed. *The Diary of James K. Polk During His Presidency, 1845–1849*. Chicago: A. C. McClurg and Co., 1910.

Royall, Anne. *Mrs. Royall's Southern Tour or Second Series of the Black Book*. Washington: N.p., 1831.

David Rumsey Map Collection, www.davidrumsey.com

Siegel, Stanley. *The Poet President of Texas: The Life of Mirabeau B. Lamar, President of the Republic of Texas.* Traverse City, MI: Jenkins Publishing Co., 1977.

Smith, Solomon Franklin. *Theatrical Management in the West and South for Thirty Years Interspersed with Anecdotical Sketches.* New York: Harper and Brothers, 1868.

Southall, Geneva Handy. *Blind Tom, the Black Pianist-Composer (1849–1908): Continually Enslaved.* Washington: Scarecrow Press, 2002.

Standard, Diffee William. *Columbus, Georgia in the Confederacy: The Social and Industrial Life of the Chattahoochee River Port.* Columbus, GA: William-Frederick Press, 1954.

Stuart, James, *Three Years in North America.* Edinburgh, Scotland: Robert Cadell, 1833.

Storey, Virginia Johnson. *The History of the Development of Public Libraries in Columbus, Georgia.* Columbus, GA: N.p., 1976.

H. S. Tanner, *The American Traveller or Guide Through the United States.* First edition is: Philadelphia: H.S. Tanner, 1834. I used a later, self-published edition.

Telfair, Nancy. *History of Columbus, 1828–1928.* Columbus, GA: Columbus Office Supply Company, 1928.

Thomas, Jr., Kenneth H. *Columbus, Georgia in Vintage Postcards.* Charleston: Arcadia Press, 2001.

Southerland, Jr., Henry deLeon, and Jerry Elijah Brown. *The Federal Road Through Georgia, the Creek Nation, and Alabama, 1806–1836.* Tuscaloosa: University of Alabama Press, 1990.

Whitehead, Margaret Laney, and Barbara Bogart. *City of Progress: A History of Columbus, Georgia.* Columbus, GA: Cosco Press, 1979.

Williams, Jack K. *Dueling in the Old South: Vignettes of Social History.* College Station: Texas A&M University Press, 1980.

Wilson, Charles Reagan, and William Ferris, eds. *Encyclopedia of Southern Culture,* Chapel Hill: University of North Carolina Press, 1989.

Wilson, Samuel, ed. *Southern Travels: Journal of John H.B. Latrobe, 1834.* New Orleans: Historic New Orleans Collection, 1986.

Willoughby, Lynn. *Fair to Middlin': The Antebellum Cotton Trade of the Apalachicola-Chattahoochee River Valley.* Tuscaloosa: University of Alabama Press, 1993.

———. *Flowing Through Time: A History of the Lower Chattahoochee Valley*. Tuscaloosa: University of Alabama Press, 1999.

Winn, William, Karol Ann Peard Lawson, and Frank T. Schnell. *Building on a Legacy: The Columbus Museum*. Columbus, GA: Columbus Museum, 1996.

Winn, William. *Line of Splendor: The Life and Times of St. Luke United Methodist Church, Columbus, Georgia 1828–2008*. Columbus, GA: St. Luke Methodist Church, 2010.

Woolfolk, Elizabeth Carrow. *Pioneers, Patriots, and Planters: First Settlers of Virginia, Kentucky, North Carolina, South Carolina, and Georgia*. Houston: Wynnton Publishing, 2004.

Worsley, Etta Blanchard, *Columbus On the Chattahoochee*. Columbus, GA: Columbus Office Supply Co., 1951.

Young, Mary Elizabeth, *Redskins, Ruffleshirts, and Rednecks: Indian Allotments in Alabama and Mississippi 1830–1860*. Norman: University of Oklahoma Press, 1961.

NOTES

1 This overview of travel writing is taken in large part from Charles Reagan Wilson and William Ferris, eds., *Encyclopedia of Southern Culture* (Chapel Hill: University of North Carolina Press, 1989) and John Cox, *Traveling South: Travel Narratives and the Construction of American Identity* (Athens: University of Georgia Press, 2005).

2 For a sense of the interest in the South and the patterns in travel writing of the period, see Thomas D. Clark, ed., *Travels in the Old South: A Bibliography* (Norman: University of Oklahoma Press, 1956).

3 Cox, *Traveling South*, 1–17; Wilson and Ferris, *Encyclopedia of Southern Culture*, 872–73.

4 This overview of the history of antebellum Columbus is largely drawn from the several most-widely available chronicles of the city's past. These include: Rita Folse Elliott, *Living in Columbus, Georgia 1828–1869: The Lives of Creeks, Traders, Enslaved African Americans, Mill Operatives and Others as Told to Archaeologists* (Columbus: City of Columbus, 2005); Roger Harris, *Our Town: An Introduction to the History of Columbus, Georgia* (Columbus: Historic Columbus Foundation, 1992); Elizabeth Evans Kilbourne, *Columbus, Georgia, Newspaper Clippings* (Savannah, GA: E.E. Kilbourne, 1997); F. Clason Kyle, *Images: A Pictorial History of Columbus, Georgia* (Norfolk, VA: Donning Co., 1986); John Lupold, *Columbus, Georgia 1828–1978* (Columbus: Columbus Sesquicentennial, 1978); John Lupold et al, *Heritage Park: A Celebration of the Industrial Heritage of Columbus, Georgia* (Columbus: Historic Columbus Foundation, 1999); Joseph B. Mahan, *Columbus: Georgia's Fall Line Trading Town* (Northridge: Windsor Publications, 1986); Katherine Hines Mahan, *Showboats to Soft Shoes: A Century of Musical Development in Columbus, Georgia, 1828–1928* (Columbus: Columbus Office Supply Co., 1968); John H. Martin, *Columbus, Georgia, From Its Selection as a Trading Town in 1827, To Its Partial Destruction by Wilson's Raid in 1865* (Columbus: Thomas

Gilbert, 1874); Nancy Telfair, *History of Columbus, 1828–1928* (Columbus: Columbus Office Supply Co., 1928); Margaret Laney Whitehead and Barbara Bogart, *City of Progress: A History of Columbus, Georgia* (Columbus: Cosco Press, 1979); Lynn Willoughby, *Flowing Through Time: A History of the Lower Chattahoochee Valley* (Tuscaloosa: University of Alabama Press, 1999); William Winn, *Line of Splendor: The Life and Times of St. Luke United Methodist Church, Columbus, Georgia 1828–2008* (Columbus: St. Luke Methodist Church, 2010); Etta Blanchard Worsley, *Columbus On the Chattahoochee* (Columbus: Columbus Office Supply Co., 1951). As many of these histories tell in similar fashion many details of the city's early history, I have in some places cited only the most succinct source for particular details that may be found in virtually all.

5 For an contextual overview of Georgia during the period of Columbus's founding, see James C. Cobb, *Georgia Odyssey: A Short History of the State* (Athens: University of Georgia Press, 2008); Kenneth L. Coleman, ed., *A History of Georgia* (Athens: University of Georgia Press, 1991); Buddy Sullivan, *Georgia: A State History* (Charleston, SC: Arcadia Press, 2003).

6 Ibid. Although the Treaty of Indian Springs ceded Creek lands in Georgia and Alabama, it aroused considerable interest because it was negotiated with only a portion of the Creek leadership and later deemed invalid. A revised treaty, which has become known as the Treaty of Washington (1826), amended its terms so that only that portion lying within the state of Georgia was ceded.

7 William C. Dawson, *A Compilation of the Laws of the State of Georgia, Passed By the General Assembly, Since the Year 1819 to the Year 1829, Inclusive* (Milledgeville, GA: Grantland and Orme, 1831) 132–33, 470–71.

8 Lupold, *Columbus Georgia*, 3; Worsley, *Columbus on the Chattahoochee*, 66–68.

9 Lupold, *Columbus Georgia*, 5; Mahan, *Columbus*, 24; Worsley, *Columbus on the Chattahoochee*, 60; Winn, *Line of Splendor*, 26.

10 Mahan, *Columbus*, 24; Worsley, *Columbus on the Chattahoochee*, 59, 64; Farris W. Cadle, *Georgia Land Surveying History and Law* (Athens: University of Georgia Press, 1991) 290–294. Truman appears to have been a nickname for Edward Lloyd Thomas's son, whose given name was Jacob. See John Goff, "Edward Lloyd Thomas, Surveyor," *Emory University Quarterly*, 18.2 (Summer, 1962), 107–119.

11 Mahan, *Columbus*, 25; Lupold, *Columbus Georgia*, ibid. 3-5; Worsley, *Columbus on the Chattahoochee*, 65; Willoughby, *Flowing Through Time*, 6. It is interesting to note that town surveyor Thomas was also hired to be secretary of the lottery. See Winn, *Line of Splendor*, 28.

12 *Notes Taken on the Survey of the Reservation at the Cowetah Falls of the Chattahoochee River, and also of the Town of Columbus*, E.L. Thomas Surveyor. Edward Lloyd Thomas Papers, Emory University Manuscript, Archives and Rare Books Library; Lupold, *Columbus Georgia*, 5; Kyle, *Images*, 21.

13 Lupold, *Columbus Georgia*, 5; Worsley, *Columbus on the Chattahoochee*, 70–72, 94; Willoughby, *Flowing Through Time*, 55; Lamar, Mirebeau *Columbus Enquirer*, 14 February 1829, 1; *Columbus Enquirer*, 4 August, 1832.

14 Mahan, *Columbus*, 32–33; unknown author, *Columbus Enquirer*, 27 February 1830, 1.

15 Worsley, *Columbus on the Chattahoochee*, 177; Kyle, *Images*, 43; *Columbus, Georgia City Directory, 1859–1860;* Kilbourne, *Columbus, Georgia, Newspaper Clippings.*

16 Lupold, *Columbus Georgia*, 24; Kyle, *Images*, 29; French and Associates, *Georgia Architectural and Historic Properties Survey: Columbus Historic District*. Found in the Files of Historic Columbus (formerly Historic Columbus Foundation).

17 Columbus State University Archives (Historical Photograph Collection).

18 Willoughby, *Flowing Through Time*, 6; Lupold, *Columbus Georgia*, 11–12; Martin, *Columbus, Georgia From Its Selection as a Trading Town*, 27–29, 76–77; Mahan, *Columbus*, 44–45.

19 Martin, *Columbus, Georgia From Its Selection as a Trading Town*, 23.

20 Telfair, *History of Columbus*, 45; Lupold, *Columbus Georgia*, 16. For more on the Apalachicola-Chattahoochee-Flint River System cotton trade, see Lynn Willoughby, *Fair to Middlin': The Antebellum Cotton Trade of the Apalachicola-Chattahoochee River Valley* (Tuscaloosa: University of Alabama Press, 1993) and Willoughby, *Flowing Through Time*.

21 Edward A. Mueller, *Perilous Journeys: A History of Steamboating on the Chattahoochee, Apalachicola, and Flint Rivers, 1828–1928* (Eufaula, AL: Historic Chattahoochee Commission, 1990);

Martin, *Columbus, Georgia From Its Selection as a Trading Town*, 117–18.

22 Mahan, *Columbus*, 31; Lupold, *Columbus Georgia*, 16; Mueller, *Perilous Journeys* 22–94; Willoughby, *Flowing Through Time*, 65–82.

23 Lupold, *Columbus Georgia*, 22; Mahan, *Columbus*, 29, 37–38. John R. deTreville, "The Little New South: Origins of Industry in Georgia's Fall-Line Cities, 1840–1865" (PhD diss., University of North Carolina Press, 1986) 83–84. Lowell, Massachusetts was founded in the 1820s as a planned manufacturing center. Within a few decades it had become home to one of the largest urban industrial complexes in the nation.

24 Mahan, *Columbus*, 38, 46; Lupold, et al., *Heritage Park*, 31–33; Telfair, *History of Columbus*, 83. Eagle Mill was the forerunner of Eagle and Phenix Mills. The paper manufactory was known as the Rock Island Paper Mill.

25 Mahan, *Columbus*, 34, 38, 42–43; Lupold, *Columbus Georgia*, 19.

26 Mahan, *Columbus*, 39, 46; Lupold, *Columbus Georgia*, 27; Whitehead, *City of Progress*, 93.

27 The best study of slavery in the region is Anthony Gene Carey, *Sold Down the River: Slavery in the Lower Chattahoochee Valley of Alabama and Georgia* (Tuscaloosa: University of Alabama Press, 2011). See also Elliott, *Living in Columbus, Georgia*.

28 For an overview of slave life in the Chattahoochee Valley during the era, see Carey, *Sold Down the River*. The structure of society in the antebellum South is well-established in numerous high-quality and readily available studies. Among the most useful are the writings of Eugene D. Genovese, especially *Roll Jordan Roll: The World the Slaves Made* (New York: Random House, 1974); *The Political Economy of Slavery: Studies in the Economy and Society of the Slave South* (Hanover, CT: Wesleyan University Press, 1989); and *The World the Slaveholders Made: Two Essays in Interpretation* (Hanover, CT: Wesleyan University Press, 1988). See also Kenneth M. Stampp, *The Peculiar Institution: Slavery in the Ante-bellum South* (New York: Random House, 1989). For an undestanding of the institution in Georgia specifically, see Watson W. Jennison, *Cultivating Race: The Expansion of Slavery in Georgia, 1750–1860* (Lexington: University of Kentucky Press, 2012.)

29 For biographical information on King, see John Lupold and Thomas L. French, Jr., *Bridging Deep South Rivers: The Life and Legend of Horace King* (Athens: University of Georgia Press, 2004).

30 Overviews of Creek history during the era are provided in several excellent studies. For an overview of the overall nation's distressed condition at the time of Columbus's founding, see Michael Green, *The Politics of Indian Removal: Creek Government and Society in Crisis* (Lincoln: University of Nebraska Press, 1985); Telfair, *History of Columbus*, 45.

31 Columbus became the focal point for fraudulent speculation in Creek lands in the 1830s, much of it carried out under the auspices of the agents of the "Columbus Land Company." The full story of Columbus's role in the saga of the Creek Removal has not yet been told. Two readily available publications on the Second Creek War era that provide important details on this story are John Ellisor's *The Second Creek War* and Mary Elizabeth Young, *Redskins, Ruffleshirts, and Rednecks: Indian Allotments in Alabama and Mississippi, 1830–1860* (Norman: University of Oklahoma Press, 1961). Billy Winn's forthcoming manuscript on Indian Removal from Georgia and Alabama, being prepared for publication at the time this book goes to press, promises to chronicle the local role in Creek Removal in greater detail than any previous study.

32 Currently the most complete chronicle of the Second Creek War is John T. Ellisor, *The Second Creek War: Interethnic Conflict and Collusion on a Collapsing Frontier* (Lincoln: University of Nebraska Press, 2010).

33 Telfair, *History of Columbus*, 92.

34 In the 1830s the Creeks, Choctaws, and Chickasaws all ceded lands west of Columbus. For an overview of these treaties and their effects on the early development of Alabama and Mississippi, see William Warren Rogers, Robert David Ward, Leah Rawls Atkins, and Wayne Flynt. *Alabama: The History of a Deep South State* (Tuscaloosa: University of Alabama Press, 1994); and Westley F. Busbee, *Mississippi: A History* (Hoboken, NJ: Wiley-Blackwell, 2005). The Mexican War has been discussed in numerous histories for its close association with the idea of "Manifest Destiny," or the rightful expansion of America's territorial claims across the width of the North American continent, and its triggering a wave of expansion-related migration from

Southern, slave-holding states. The most recent of these is Amy S. Greenberg, *A Wicked War: Polk, Clay, Lincoln and the 1846 U.S. Invasion of Mexico* (New York: Random House, 2012). Information on Fannin from Beryl I. Diamond, "James Walker Fannin, Jr.," *New Georgia*, www.georgiaencyclopedia.org/articles/government-politics/james-walker-fannin-jr-1804-1836. For biographical information on Lamar and his remarkable story, see Jack C. Ramsay, *Thunder Beyond the Brazos: Mirabeau B. Lamar, a Biography* (Fort Worth, TX: Eakin Press, 1984); and Stanley Siegel, *The Poet President of Texas: The Life of Mirabeau B. Lamar, President of the Republic of Texas* (Traverse City MI: Jenkins Publishing Co., 1977). Lupold, *Columbus Georgia*, 11; Martin, *Columbus, Georgia From Its Selection as a Trading Town*, 128; Worsley, *Columbus on the Chattahoochee*, 182.

35 For biographical information on early states' rights leaders in Columbus, see Worsley, *Columbus on the Chattahoochee.* Crawford served in Congress before the Civil War and became an outspoken advocate of states' rights, and during the war he served in the Confederate Provisional Congress and as a Confederate Commissioner to the United States; Bethune published the *Corner Stone*, one of the earliest Southern newspapers to argue consistently for the immediate secession of the Southern states; Benning became a leading proponent of states' rights and secession during his career as a lawyer and judge, and is most remembered for his distinguished service in the Confederate Army; Walter T. Colquitt served as a vocal advocate of Southern rights and slavery as a United States Senator, and attended the 1850 Nashville Convention that debated the issue of secession; his son Alfred Colquitt served in Congress and attended the Georgia Secession Convention before serving in the Confederate Army; younger brother Peyton became a local military leader with the City Light Guards before the Civil War, and achieved fame for his service during the conflict.

36 See Martin, *Columbus, Georgia From Its Selection as a Trading Town*. For information on the early days of Girard, see *The Heritage of Russell County, Alabama*. (Clanton, AL: Heritage Publishing Consultants, 2003); and Russell County Historical Commission, *The History of Russell County, Alabama* (Dallas, TX: National ShareGraphics, 1982).

37 Laurence Eugene O'Keeffe Diary, Columbus State University Archives mc 218; Martin, *Columbus, Georgia From Its Selection as a Trading Town*, 67, 132.

38 Martin, *Columbus, Georgia From Its Selection as a Trading Town*, 33; Lupold, *Columbus Georgia*, 9; Jack K. Williams, *Dueling in the Old South: Vignettes of Social History* (College Station: Texas A&M University Press, 1980) 54. As if to underscore the violent nature of Southern society at the time of Columbus's birth, it should be noted that after Camp killed Woolfolk in their duel, he was in turn gunned down in a Columbus street. See Winn, *Line of Splendor*, 37.

39 For a sampling of reported causes of death of citizens year by year in Columbus newspapers, see Martin, *Columbus, Georgia From Its Selection as a Trading Town*; and Mary Jane Galer, *Columbus, Georgia Lists of People, 1828–1852 and Sexton's Reports to 1866* (Columbus, GA: Iberian Publishing Company, 2000).

40 Lupold, *Columbus Georgia*, 15; Mahan, *Columbus*, 48; James J. Gilbert: *A History of the First Presbyterian Church of Columbus, Georgia* (Columbus GA: Gilbert Printing Company, 1930); Winn, *Line of Splendor*.

41 Winn, *Line of Splendor*, 44–45, 57, 59–60; Martin, *Columbus, Georgia From Its Selection as a Trading Town*, 20; Worsley, *Columbus on the Chattahoochee*, 177; Lupold, *Columbus Georgia*, 14.

42 Martin, *Columbus, Georgia From Its Selection as a Trading Town*, 29, 100; Lupold; *Columbus Georgia*, 14, 16; Worsley, *Columbus on the Chattahoochee*, 90. Local legend maintains an early druggist may have actually established the first free lending library of sorts by loaning customers books from a back room in his store. See Virginia Johnson Storey, *The History of the Development of Public Libraries in Columbus, Georgia* (Columbus, GA: n.p., 1976); Katherine Hines Mahan and William C. Woodall, *A History of Public Education in Muscogee County and the City of Columbus, Georgia, 1828–1976* (Columbus, GA: Muscogee County Board of Education, 1977) 6–38.

43 William Winn, Karol Ann Peard Lawson, and Frank T. Schnell, *Building on a Legacy: The Columbus Museum* (Columbus GA: Columbus Museum, 1996) 10. For information on the American Art-Union, see Mary Bartlett Cowdrey, *American Academy of Fine Arts and American Art-Union, 1816–1852: With a History of the American Academy* (New York: New York Historical Society, 1953).

44 Lupold, *Columbus Georgia*, 12.

45 Winn, et al., *Building on a Legacy*, 9. For biographical information on Wiggins see Deirdre O'Connell, The Ballad of Blind Tom, Slave Pianist. New York: Overlook Press, 2009 and Geneva Handy Southall, Blind Tom, the Black Pianist-Composer (1849–1908): Continually Enslaved. Washington: Scarecrow Press, 2002. Katherine Hines. *Showboats to Soft Shoes: A Century ASSINGof Musical Development in Columbus, Georgia, 1828–1928*. Columbus: Columbus Office Supply Company, 1968, 2–26.

46 Worsley, *Columbus on the Chattahoochee*, 73; Martin, *Columbus, Georgia From Its Selection as a Trading Town*, 13; Lupold, *Columbus Georgia*, 12, 14, Mahan, *Columbus*, 49. Mahan, Hines. *Showboats to Soft Shoes*, ibid.

47 Hines, *Showboats to Soft Shoes*, ibid.; Telfair, *History of Columbus*, 92; Kyle, *Images*, 23, Lupold, *Columbus Georgia*, 9; Winn, et al., *Building on a Legacy*, 9; Martin, *Columbus, Georgia From Its Selection as a Trading Town*, 140.

48 Martin, *Columbus, Georgia From Its Selection as a Trading Town*, 37–38; Kyle, Images, 22; O'Keefe Diary, Columbus State University Archives.

49 Biographical information on Thomas taken from John Goff, "Edward Lloyd Thomas, Surveyor," *Emory University Quarterly*, 18.2 (Summer, 1962), 107–119.

50 *Notes Taken on the Survey of the Reservation at the Cowetah Falls of the Chattahoochee River, and also of the Town of Columbus*, E.L. Thomas Surveyor, Columbus State University Archives.

51 Ibid., 7 February 1828; 29 January, 1828.

52 Ibid., 30 January 1828.

53 Ibid., 16 February 1828; 7 February 1828.

54 Ibid., 8, 9, 11, 20, 21 February 1828.

55 Ibid., 25 February 1828; 3 April 1828.

56 Ibid., 27 February 1828; 8, 11, 16, 17 March 1828. The house where Truman was taken to is reputedly contained within what is now the Thomas-Kivline-Wolhwender House at 808 Broadway.

57 Ibid., 28 March 1828; 11, 21, 23, 24 April 1828.

58 See Basil Hall, *Travels in North America, in the Years 1827 and 1828* (Edinburgh, Scotland: Cadell and Co., 1829). His account of his visit to Columbus is contained in pages 280–87. For biographical information on Hall, see John Burke, *The Royal Families* *of England, Scotland, and Wales, with Their Descendants, Sovereigns and Subject* (London: E. Churton, 1851); John Martine and E.J. Wilson, eds., *Reminiscences and Notices of Ten Parishes of the County of Haddington* (Haddington, Scotland: William Sinclair, 1894); Sidney Lee, ed, *Dictionary of National Biography: Index and Epitome* (London: Smith, Elder, and Co. 1903). Hall's other publications include *An Account of a Voyage of Discovery to the West Coast of Corea, and the Great Loo-Choo Island* (Philadelphia: Abraham Small, 1818) and *Extracts from a Journal Written on the Coasts of Chili, Peru and Mexico, in the Years 1820, 1821, 1822* (Edinburgh, Scotland: Archibald Constable and Co., 1824).

59 Hall, *Travels in North America*, 280, 283. Though patented in 1806, the camera lucida was essentially an advanced version of a device invented by Johannes Kepler almost two hundred years earlier. The camera utilized a prism to reflect a scene onto a drawing surface in a way that allowed the artist to see both his subject and the drawing surface simultaneously. This technique allowed the scene to be "traced," facilitating a remarkably accurate representation.

60 Ibid., 287.

61 Ibid. 280–287.

62 Una Pope Hennessey, *The Aristocratic Journey: Being the Outspoken Letters of Mrs. Basil Hall Written during a Fourteen Months' Sojourn in America, 1827–1828.* New York: Putnam, 1931. Mrs. Hall's chronicle of her visit to Columbus is contained in pages 238–239.

63 "The Town of Columbus," *Milledgeville Recorde*r, 2 August 1828. This is from the Digital Library's Newspaper Collection, Milledgeville Historic Newspaper Archiv. http://milledgeville.galieleo.uss.edu/milledgeville/season.

64 Ibid. The *Recorder* began publication in 1820 and continued until the 1870s, eventually merging with another publication that continues to this day. Milledgeville served as Georgia's capital from 1804 to 1868.

65 A potential rival city in the form of the small community of Girard, already occupied the western bank of the Chattahoochee opposite of Columbus. The village did not grow at the same pace as Columbus, and remained something of a suburb of the Georgia city throughout the antebellum period.

66 Anne Royall, *Mrs. Royall's Southern Tour or Second Series of the Black Book* (Washington: N.p., 1831) 138–41.

67 For biographical information on Royall, see Alice S. Maxwell and Marion B. Dunlevy, *Virago! The Story of Anne Newport Royall* (Jefferson, NC: McFarland, 1985) and George Stuyvesant Jackson, *Uncommon Scold: The Story of Anne Royall* (Boston: Bruce Humphries, 1937). Royall had already published an account of a visit to the South prior to her arrival in Columbus: *Letters From Alabama* (Washington: N.p., 1830). Her other writings include: *Sketches of History, Life and Manners in the United States, by a Traveller* (New Haven, CT: "For the author," 1826); *The Tennessean, a novel founded on fact* (New Haven, CT: "For the author," 1827); *The Black Book, a Continuation of Travels in the United States* (Washington: "For the author," 1828–29); *Mrs. Royall's Pennsylvania, or Travels in the United States* (Washington: "For the author," 1829); *Paul Pry* (Washington, "For the author," 1831–36); *The Huntress* (Washington, "For the author," 1836–54.

68 It is likely that the Mr. Van Ness to whom Royall refers is James Van Ness, Intendant for Columbus in 1829.

69 Edwin L. deGraffenreid served as one of the original commissioners for the planning of the city of Columbus.

70 While it is safe to assume all the gentlemen named in Royall's account were relatively prominent citizens of Columbus at the time of her visit, only a few can be identified with certainty. J.C. Hall, David Britt and Jacob I. Moses were all key players in the formation of some of Columbus's early militia units, and George W. Dillard was the proprietor of the Globe Tavern and later served as a city commissioner.

71 James Stuart, *Three Years in North America*, volume 2 (Edinburgh, Scotland: Robert Cadell, 1833) 161–66.

72 Biographical information taken from Leslie Stephen and Sidney Lee, eds., *Dictionary of National Biography*, (Vol. LV London: Smith, Elder and Co., 1898) 90–92.

73 Stuart, *Three Years in North America*, 161–66.

74 Solomon Franklin Smith, *Theatrical Management in the West and South for Thirty Years Interspersed with Anecdotical Sketches* (New York: Harper and Brothers, 1868) 78–80. For more on the genre of writing known as "Old Southwest humor," see Hennig Cohen and William B. Dillingham, eds., *Humor of the Old South-*

west (Athens: University of Georgia Press, 1982) and Nancy L. Griffith, *Humor of the Old Southwest: An Annotated Bibliography of Primary and Secondary Sources* (Bloomington: Indiana University Press, 1989).

75 Biographical information on Smith taken from Charles Watson, "Sol Smith," *Encyclopedia of Alabama*, http://www.encyclopediaofalabama.org/face/Article.jsp?id=h-2423.

76 Smith, *Theatrical Management*, 78–80.

77 C. D. Arfwedson, *The United States and Canada, in 1832, 1833, and 1834* (London: Richard Bentley, 1834) 1–9. Biographical information taken from Herman Hofberg, ed., *Swedish Biographical Hand Dictionary* (Stockholm: Bonniers, 1906).

78 The name "Sodom" appears to have been a locally popular name of derision given to the frontier community of Girard in reference to its being a supposedly wild and lawless community located within the bounds Creek territory. Much of Arfwedson's commentary on the community must be taken with a grain of salt, as it was no doubt influenced by conversations with locals. Even by the standards of frontier towns in the South during this era, however, Girard appears to have been a place of violence that many criminals did retreat to in order to be somewhat out of reach of immediate legal authority.

79 Arfwedson, *The United States and Canada*, 1–9.

80 Tyrone Power, *Impressions of America During the Years 1833, 1834, and 1835* (Philadelphia: Carey, Lea and Blanchard, 1836) 86–90. Perhaps the most well-known of Power's plays is *How to Pay the Rent.* Biographical information taken from Montrose Jonas Moses, *Famous Actor-Families in America* (New York: T.Y. Crowell and Co., 1906).

81 Smith mistakenly described the Creek or Yuchi people he encountered as "Choctaw."

82 Power, *Impressions*, 86–90.

83 Biographical information taken from Samuel Wilson, Jr., ed., *Southern Travels: Journal of John H.B. Latrobe, 1834* (New Orleans: Historic New Orleans Collection, 1986). The legal book Latrobe wrote is *The Justice's Practice Under the Laws of Maryland.* Latrobe later published a history of Maryland's involvement with the African Colonization Society, *Maryland in Africa* (Baltimore: John Murphy and Co., 1885).

84 Wilson, ed., *Southern Travels.*

85 The steamer *Van Buren* began service on the Chattahoochee in 1833 and was destroyed by fire on the night of December 5, 1834 while tied up at a landing south of Columbus; see Mueller, *Perilous Journeys*, 26–28.

86 George William Featherstonhaugh, *Excursion Through the Slave States* (London: John Murray, 1844) 319–21. After his pioneering work with the US government, Featherstonhaugh later served as British consul to France. His other publications include *Report of a Geological Reconnaissance made in 1835 from the Seat of Government by the way of Green Bay and the Wisconsin Territory to the Coteau du Prairie, an Elevated Ridge Dividing the Missouri from the Saint Peters River* (Washington: Gales and Seaton, 1836) and, *A Canoe Voyage up the Minnay Sotar* (London: Richard Bentley, 1847). For biographical information, see Edmund Berkeley and Dorothy Smith Berkeley. *George William Featherstonhaugh: The First U.S. Government Geologist* (Tuscaloosa: University of Alabama Press, 1988).

87 Harriet Martineau, *Society in America* (Paris: Baudry's European Library 1837) 147–49.

88 Martineau's writings include *Illustrations of Political Economy* (London: Charles Fox, 1834); *Retrospect of Western Travel* (London: Saunders and Otley, 1838); *Eastern Life Present and Past* (Philadelphia: Lea and Blanchard, 1848); *How to Observe Morals and Manner* (London: Charles Knight and Co., 1838). For biographical information, see Susan Hoecker-Drysdale, *Harriet Martineau: First Woman Sociologist* (New York: Berg, 1992); Valerie Kossew Pichanick, *Harriet Martineau: The Woman and Her Work, 1802–76* (Ann Arbor: University of Michigan Press, 1980); Deborah Anna Logan, *The Hour and the Woman: Harriet Martineau's "Somewhat Remarkable" Life* (Dekalb: Northern Illinois University Press. 2002).

89 Martineau, *Society in America*, 147–49.

90 James S. Buckingham, *The Slave States of America* (London: Fisher, Son and Co., 1842) 243–49. Buckingham quote from preface. Buckingham edited for several newspapers in addition to authoring *Travels in Palestine Through the Countries of Bashan and Gilead, East of the River Jordan, Including a Visit to the Cities of Geraza and Gamala in the Decapolis* (London: Longman, Hurst, Rees, Orme, and Brown) 1822 and *Travels among the Arab Tribes Inhabiting the Countries East of Syria and Palestine* (London: Longman, Hurst, Rees, Orme, and Green) 1825. Biographical information taken from G. F. R. Barker, "Buckingham, James Silk (1786–1855)," rev. Felix Driver, *Oxford Dictionary of National Biography* (Oxford: Oxford University Press, 2004) www.oxford dnb.com/view/article/3855.

91 Ibid.

92 How exactly Buckingham arrived at the erroneous conclusion that Columbus was settled "chiefly" by settlers from New England is unknown, but the city did have several prominent families with ancestors from the Northeast to whom he may have been introduced. The bulk of Columbus's 1830 population hailed from elsewhere in Georgia and, in smaller numbers, from the states of Virginia, North Carolina, and South Carolina.

93 The portrait Buckingham refers to was probably a copy of the full-length one of Creek chief William McIntosh. Like many American Indian leaders of the era in the South, McIntosh had both European and American Indian ancestry; his father was Scottish trader and his mother a Creek woman. McIntosh had been killed in 1825 by his fellow tribesmen for selling the Creek lands on which Columbus would eventually be located against tribal decree in the original Treaty of Indian Springs (1825), and privately profiting to boot. Buckingham evidently misunderstood that compact to be the Treaty of Cusseta (1832), which more directly is associated with the Second Creek War of 1836–37. The fact that Buckingham jumbles these events in his narrative is in one way an indication of the widely recognized related nature of these events, even at the time.

94 Accounts of the role of Columbus citizens in defrauding the Creeks had been printed in several places, and as far away as New York City the reputation of Columbus was disparaged by some.

95 Buckingham, *The Slave States of America,* 243–49.

96 Charles Lyell, *A Second Visit to the United States of North America* (London: John Murray, 1849) 31–35. Biographical sketch based on *Encyclopædia Britannica Online,* s. v. "Sir Charles Lyell, Baronet," http://www.britannica.com/EBchecked/topic/352672/Sir-Charles-Lyell-Baronet (accessed 25 February 2014).

97 Lyell's other writings include: *Principles of Geology* (London: John Murray, 1830); *Elements of Geology* (London: John Murray, 1838); *Geological Evidences of the Antiquity of Man* (London: John Murray, 1863); *Travels in North America* (London: John Murray, 1845).

98 The Dr. Boykin referenced here may be James Boykin, whose home, "Rose Hill" gave its name to a historic Columbus neighborhood. "Mr. Pond" may be Dr. Asa Pond, a doctor who was prominent in civic affairs and who, at one time, served as Columbus's "City Physician." Snake Shoals is located about thirty miles below Columbus.

99 The physical removal of the Creek Indians from the lower Chattahoochee Valley was a decades-long saga. While "voluntary" and forced migrations of Creeks occurred in the decade prior to Lyell's visit, a remnant of the Creek tribe managed to evade deportation for many years, and in some cases altogether, by hiding out or blending in with white society. The details surrounding the deportation Lyell references here, which is well after the mass exodus from the region in the late 1830s, are unknown at this time.

100 Lyell, *A Second Visit to the United States of North America*, 31–35.

101 Alexander Mackay, *The Western World: Travels in the United States in 1846–47* (London: Richard Bentley, 1849) 260–64. Biographical information taken from Sidney Lee, ed, *Dictionary of National Biography: Index and Epitome* (London: Smith, Elder, and Co. 1903) 117–18. Mackay's other publications include *The Crisis in Canada: or Vindication of Lord Elgin and his Cabinet* (London: James Ridgway, 1849); *Analysis of the Australian Colonies' Government Bill* (London: Ridgway, 1850); *Western India: Reports addressed to the Chambers of Commerce of Manchester, Liverpool, Blackburn, and Glasgow*. (London: Nathaniel Cooke, Milford House, Strand, 1853).

102 There are numerous good biographies of Polk readily available. One of the most recent, and best, is Walter R. Borneman's *Polk: The Man Who Transformed the Presidency and America* (New York: Random House, 2008). Polk died on 15 June 1849, shortly after visiting Columbus apparently having contracted cholera during the tour.

103 Attorney Seaborn Jones served as aide-de-camp to Georgia Governor George M. Troup prior to moving to Columbus. He quickly became one of the young community's most influential citizens, serving as president of the Bank of Columbus and as a representative in Congress.

104 James Knox Polk, *The Diary of James K. Polk During His Presidency, 1845–1849*, ed. Milo Milton Quaife (Chicago: A.C. McClurg and Co., 1910) 391–94.

105 Frederick Law Olmsted, *A Journey in the Seaboard Slave States with Remarks on Their Economy* (New York: Dix and Edwards, 1856) 548–49. Olmsted quote from preface, ix.

106 Olmsted later published an abridged version of his writings based on his travels across the South as *The Cotton Kingdom: A Traveller's Observations on Cotton and Slavery In the American Slave States* (Mason Brothers: New York, 1862).

107 Olmstead, *A Journey in the Seaboard Slave States*, 548–49.

INDEX